COTSWOLD *Images*

Upper Cam

COTSWOLD *Images*

——ALAN SUTTON and JOHN HUDSON——

ALAN SUTTON
1988

Alan Sutton Publishing
Brunswick Road · Gloucester

First published 1988

British Library Cataloguing in Publication Data

Cotswold, images.
  1. England. Cotswolds. Description & travel.
  1400–1980
  I. Sutton, Alan *1949*– II. Hudson, John
  914.24′17′04

  ISBN 0-86299-511-6

*Front Cover: The Cotswold edge below Stroud, looking across the River
Severn horshoe bend to the Forest of Dean and Wales.*
Photograph: Robert Carr.

Back Cover: The south Cotswold village of Castle Combe.
Photograph: Roy Nash.

Typesetting and origination by Alan Sutton Publishing Limited.
Photoset Bembo 11/13
Colour and duotones, Spa Graphics Limited, Cheltenham.
Printed in Great Britain by the Guernsey Press Company Limited.

Introduction

The Cotswold Hills: are they bare or wooded, beautiful or ugly, cosy or bleak, rich or poor?

Read contemporary accounts over the centuries, from the first references to the name in the Middle Ages to the beginning of the last war, and you will discover that they are all of the above and a great deal more. Even today, while few would describe them as ugly or poor, those who know the hills are well aware that theirs is a complex character, far removed from the blandness of the jigsaw-puzzle and the chocolate-box.

Part of it, of course, is geographical, with the wide open spaces of the northern hills contrasting with the wooded valleys of Stroud and the escarpment communities to the south. But more than that, our impressions of places are subjective, the more so if we are perceptive strangers with no preconceived notions, and it is this book's aim to record just some of those impressions or images as they were committed to paper while still fresh in the observer's mind.

The Oxford English Dictionary's first recorded instance of 'Cotswold' comes from a Latin entry in the Rolls of Parliament for 1306: 'Ecclesie de Newenton super Coteswalde'. What is not surmised in the dictionary is that the word is derived from the Saxon 'cote' for sheep-fold and 'wold' for bare hill, but that strikes us as at least a reasonable assumption.

Our images in words are accompanied by the visual images of nineteenth-century sepia photographs, engravings and late twentieth-century colour pictures of this beautiful and distinct region of England. The contemporary writings are arranged in chronological sequence and come from political tracts, diaries, letters, memoranda, official reports, business papers, topographical works and semi-fiction. Most are from published sources, but it is fair to say that many were not originally written with publication in mind. In fact when members of the Cely family wrote their letters during the Wars of the Roses, Caxton was still busy setting up his press. Cobbett obviously had an eye to posterity, and it must be asked why Francis Witts wrote in so graphic a fashion if his diary really was intended for his eyes only.

The Cotswolds' geographical area is sometimes stretched to include the entire limestone belt that runs from Dorset north-eastwards through to Lincolnshire, with Stamford in the latter county often cited as a classic Cotswold town. Our definition is much more limited and, we believe, more true to most people's acceptance of the term. Its boundaries are loosely within the four corners framed by Wotton-under-Edge to Badminton in the south-west, Cricklade to Lechlade in the south-east, Chipping Norton to Chipping Campden in the north-east and Gloucester to Broadway in the north-west. This area is almost entirely in Gloucestershire, but with fringes of Wiltshire, Oxfordshire and Worcestershire.

Strictly speaking, Gloucester and Cheltenham should be excluded as they lie in the Severn Vale, but Gloucester is important to the western Cotswolds as the county town and main shopping centre, and Cheltenham has had an

Smart's Shop, Chalford

Sezincote

influence that extends well beyond its shops and places of entertainment. For long it was famous for sucking in retired colonels and civil servants from British India, and puffing chaises full of them out in weekend parties to view the rustics in the fields from beneath their parasols. Today an abiding feature of Cotswold life is the area's popularity as a retirement place for comfortably-off military people and civil servants, and there is little doubt that the Cheltenham factor plays its part in that. In fact until recently the signs as you entered Cheltenham Spa wel-

comed you to 'The Centre for the Cotswolds'. Since then the Trade Descriptions Act has presumably taken its toll, for the signs have latterly been replaced by a more modest claim.

This book is a collection of comments and impressions by visitors to the Cotswolds, mixed with the day-to-day business of farmers, rectors, merchants and even the occasional dilettante who, like many before and since, has left the city behind to be the 'first to discover life' west of Oxford.

COTSWOLD *Images*

Our first selection dates from 1471, shortly after the Yorkist Edward IV had deposed Henry VI for the second time by defeating the Lancastrians at the Battle of Tewkesbury. This is an 'official' account of the battle sent to the citizens of Bruges in the Low Countries, to whom Edward owed no small debt for his success. The account takes up after the Battle of Barnet, when the Lancastrian army was trying to cross the Severn to meet up with reinforcements in Wales and Edward's Yorkists were in hot pursuit.

Our extract begins on the morning of 3 May 1471, with Edward camped outside Chipping Sodbury and Henry's queen, Margaret of Anjou and her son Edward, Prince of Wales, camped at Berkeley Castle. Henry himself had already been captured and was imprisoned in the Tower. This partial text is in the original spelling, which is relatively easy to follow:

HISTORIE OF THE ARRIVALL OF EDWARD IV IN ENGLAND AND THE FINALL RECOUERYE OF HIS KINGDOMES FROM HENRY VI A.D. MCCCCLXXI

Early in the mornynge, soone aftar three of the cloke, the Kynge had certayne tydyngs that they [*the enemy*] had taken theyre way by Barkley toward Gloucestar. Whereupon he toke advise of his counsell of that he had to doo for the stopynge of theyr wayes, at two passagys afore namyd, by Gloucestar, or els by Tewkesberye. And, first, he purvayed for Gloucestar, and sent thethar certayne servaunts of his owne to Richard Bewchamp, sonne and heyr to the Lord Bewchampe, to whom afore he had comyttyd the rule and govarnaunce of the towne and castell of Gloucestar, commaundynge hym to kepe the towne and castle for the Kynge, and that he, with suche helpe as he myght have, shuld defend the same agaynst them, in caas they woulde in any wise assayle them, as it was suppos they so would doo that same aforenone.

And, yf he mygt know that they so dyde, he promised to come to theyr rescows, and comforte. With this the Kyngs message they were well receyved at Gloucestar, and the towne and castell put in sure and save kepinge of the sayd Richard, and the sayde Kynges servaunts. Whiche message was sent and done in right good season, for certayne it is the Kynges enemyes were put in sure hope, and determyned to have enteryd the towne, and ethar have kept it agaynst the Kynge, or, at the leaste, to have passed thrwghe the towne into othar contries, where they thowght [*to*] have bene myghtely assysted.

For which cawses they had greatly travayled theyr people all that nyght and mornynge, upon the Fryday, to about ten of the cloke they were comen afore Gloucestar; where there entent was uttarly denyed them by Richard Bewchampe, and othar of the Kyngs servaunts, that, for that cawse, the Kynge had sent thethar. And, therefore, they shortly toke theyr conclusyon for to go the next way to Tewkesbery, whithar they came the same day, about four aftar none. By whiche tyme they hadd so travaylled theyr hoaste by nyght and daye that they were ryght wery for travaylynge; for by that tyme they had travaylyd xxxvj [*thirty-six*] longe myles, in a fowle contrye, all in lanes and

Condicote Lane

A Cotswold barn near Northleach

stonny wayes, betwyxt woodes, without any good refresshynge.

So, whethar it were of theyr election and good will or no, but that they were veryly compelled to byde by two cawses; one was, for werines of theyr people, which they supposed nat theyr people woulde have eny longer endured; an other, for they knew well that the Kynge ever approchyd towards them, nere and nere, evar redy, in good aray and ordinaunce, to have pursuyd and fallen uppon them, yf they wolde any ferther have gon, and, paradventure, to theyr moste dyssavantage.

They therefore determyned t'abyde there th'aventure that God would send them in the qwarell they had taken in hand. And, for that entent, the same nyght they pight them in a fielde, in a close even at the townes ende; the towne, and the abbey, at theyr backs; afore them, and upon every hand of them, fowle lanes, and depe dikes, and many hedges, with hylls, and valleys, a ryght evill place to approche, as cowlde well have bene devysed.

The Kynge, the same mornynge, the Fryday, erly, avanced his banners, and devyded his hole hoost in three battayles, and sent afore hym his forydars, and scorars, on every syde hym, and so, in fayre arraye and ordinaunce, he toke his way thrwghe the champain contrye, callyd Cotteswolde, travylynge all his people, whereof were moo than iij M [*3,000*] fotemen, that Fryday, which was right-an-hot day, xxx myle and more; whiche his people might nat finde, in all the way, horse-mete, ne mansmeate, ne so moche as drynke for theyr horses.

And all that day was evarmore the Kyngs hoste within v or vj myles of his enemyes; he in playne contry and they amongst woods; havynge allway good espialls upon them. So, continuynge that journey he came, with all his hooste, to a village callyd Chiltenham, but five myles from Tewkesberye, where the Kynge had certayn knolege that, but litle afore his comynge thethar, his enemyes were comen to Tewkesbury, and there were takynge a field,

wherein they purposed to abyde, and delyver him battayle. Whereupon the Kynge made no longar taryenge, but a litle confortyd hymselfe, and his people, with suche meate and drynke as he had done to be caried with hym, for vitalyge of his hooste; and, incontinent, set forthe towards his enemyes, and toke the fielde, and lodgyd hym selfe, and all his hooste, within three myle of them.

Upon the morow followynge, Saterday, the iiij day of May, the Kynge apparailed hymselfe, and all his hoost set in good array; ordeined three wards; displayed his bannars; dyd blowe up the trompets; commytted his caws and qwarell to Almyghty God, to owr most blessyd lady his mothar, Vyrgyn Mary, the glorious martyr Seint George, and all the saynts; and avaunced, directly upon his ene-myes; approchinge to theyr filde, whiche was strongly in a marvaylows strong grownd pyght, full difficult to be assayled.

Here we leave Edward and his faithful younger brother Richard, Duke of Gloucester – later to become Richard III – to win the battle, kill Edward, Prince of Wales and capture his mother, Margaret of Anjou. What a marvellous image is conjured up, though, of the king and his men, in fayre arraye and ordinaunce, advancing irrevocably over that champain contrye callyd Cotteswolde.

Still in Edward IV's reign we have the written account of England's first antiquary. William Worcestre was born in 1415, a man of wide knowledge of many subjects and a devouring curiosity about places, buildings, history and natural science. He made several journeys through England, Scotland and Wales. Today it is sometimes easy to see him as a rather naive witness, one all too ready to swallow all sorts of fanciful nonsense fed to him, either in good faith or perhaps for fun, by the folks he met along the way.

Nevertheless, he made a valuable contribution to our knowledge of English social history, and pioneered a study more successfully taken up by Leland and Camden. His comments on

the Cotswolds are few, and as his writings are in Latin these extracts, made from notes on his visit beginning on 19 August 1480, are modern translations.

Cirencester

The parish church of St. [*John the Baptist*] in the town of Cisseter, otherwise Cirencester, is 90 paces [*158 feet*] long including the choir, and its width, with the two aisles, is 50 paces [*91 feet*]. The length of the belfry of the church is 7 yards, and the width of the tower, which has no spire, is 6½ yards.

The source of the first spring of the River Thames is close to Cirencester; it rises 3 miles from the town of Tetbury in Gloucestershire at Kemble, at a chapel called Ewen in that parish, and this spring never dries up in the greatest drought.

Coates Town, from which the Cotswold Hills take their name, is 3 miles from Cirencester towards Bristol, near the Fosse Way.

Cirencester was called the city of sparrows because a certain Africanus, who came from Africa, destroyed the city after a siege by sending birds flying over the city with wildfire tied to their tails.

This last anecdote and the astonishing throwaway line: 'Grimond's Castle is another castle in Cirencester where King Arthur was crowned, near the Chapel of St. Cecilia's the Virgin, on the opposite, west, side of the town,' are telling examples of Worcestre's credulity – unless, of course, he happens to be right, and we scoff at what we cannot bring ourselves to believe! There are certainly people in the Cotswolds today who make an intriguing case for setting the Arthurian legend in this part of the world, with its easy access across the Severn to Merlin's Wales, rather than farther south in Somerset.

It is interesting that Worcestre places the source of the Thames at what we now know as Thames Head rather than at Seven

Calmsden

Cowley

Springs, and his Cirencester/Ciceter comments are a reminder that that debate goes back a few centuries. It is odd how Ciceter, which is surely no more than a rustic dialect corruption, has somehow been dignified as the 'correct' pronunciation in some people's view, and the fact that many of these people have never visited the place makes the phenomenon even odder. Meanwhile, the locals happily go on calling it Cirencester or Ciren–Zoiren, we suppose, if you want to be completely 'correct'.

Worcestre is surely wrong in his Coates/Cotswold assertion, though it could suggest that the medieval pronunciation was perhaps closer to 'Coatswold'. After all, if the name does derive from the Saxon cote, as in sheep-cote or dove-cote, both pronunciations are still acceptable today.

In November 1479 Worcestre copied notes out of a chronicle by one Brewster, who lived with Richard Beauchamp, Earl of Warwick:

Gloucester

Claudius gave his daughter Gowysya to King Arviragus of the Britons in marriage, and in memory of the celebration of this wedding built a city which he called Claudia Cestria between Leogria and Demicia on the bank of the Severn, at the time that the Apostle Peter founded the Church of Antioch.

Also contemporary with Edward IV and William Worcestre but far from whimsical and nonsensical we have the correspondence of the Cely family. The Celys were London merchants and their correspondence, now in the Public Record Office, survived through a dispute in 1489 between Richard Cely the younger and the widow of his brother George over debts arising from the brothers' joint trading ventures. The matter was taken to the Court of Chancery, and a mass of family letters and memoranda was collected as evidence. Our interest in the family arises from their Northleach connection. The brothers spent a great deal of time in the Cotswolds buying wool, and in Calais selling it. In 1482 Richard was looking for a wife, and on May Day he was shown an eligible young lady while at matins in Northleach Church . . .

This is a simplified transcript of Richard's letter to George in Calais on 13 May 1482:

Right dearly and well beloved brother, I recommend me heartily unto you, informing you at the making of this letter that our mother, brother, my godfather and the household are in good health, thanked be the Good Lord.

Sir, the same day that I departed into Cotswold I received a letter from you written at Calais the 14th April, wherein I find the inventory of such goods that would be our father's, and money, on that side of the sea.

Sir, I spoke not with the bishop's officers since I received your letter. When I spoke last with them they said that all things should await your coming. I understand by your letter that you will make over £500.

I have been in Cotswold this three weeks, and packed with William Midwinter 22 sarpliers [*a sack of 728lb weight*] and a poke [*a small sack*], whereof be 4 middle. William Bretten says it is the fairest wool that he saw this year, and I packed 4 sarpliers at Campden of the same bargain, whereof are 2 good, 2 middle.

There will be in all, with blottys [*sacks less than 364lb weight*], upon 27 or 28 sarpliers of wool. Sir, I cannot have William Midwinter's fells [*sheepskins*] under £3 10s 0d the hundred, and I shall go to that price.

I pray you send me a letter shortly. Sir, I have bought in Cotswold upon the point of 7,000 reasonably good fells, and I pay £3, I can get none under.

The same day that I came to Northleach, on a Sunday before matins from Burford, William Midwinter welcomed me, and in our communication he asked me if I were in any way of marriage. I told him nay, and he informed me that there was a young gentlewoman whose father's name is Limrick, and her mother is dead, and she shall dispend [*have as income*] by her mother £40 a year, as they say in that country, and there have been great gentlemen to see her and would have her, etc.

And before matins were done, William Midwinter had moved [*broached*] this matter to the greatest man about the gentleman Limrick, and he said and informed the aforesaid of all the matter, and the young gentlewoman both; and the Saturday after, William Midwinter went to London, as all wool gatherers were sent for by writ by the men of Pettit, for inwinding and great marking, and they have day to come again at Michaelmas.

When I had packed at Campden, and William Midwinter departed, I came to Northleach again to make an end of packing, and on the Sunday next after, the same man that William Midwinter first told of this matter came to me and told me that he had broken to his master according as Midwinter desired him, and he said his master was right well pleased therewith.

And the same man said to me if I would tarry May Day I should have a sight of the young gentlewoman, and I said I would tarry with a good will, and the same day her father should have been sitting at Northleach for the King, but he sent one of his clerks and rode himself to Winchcombe.

And to matins the same day came the young gentlewoman and her mother-in-law [*stepmother*], and I and William Bretton were saying matins when they came into church, and when matins was done they went to a kinswoman of the young gentlewoman; and I sent to them a pottell [*half-a-gallon*] of white Romnay [*sweet wine*], and they took it thankfully, for they had come a mile on foot that morning.

And when mass was done I came and welcomed them, and kissed them, and they thanked me for the wine, and prayed me to come to dinner with them, and I excused me and they made me promise to drink with them after dinner. And I sent them to dinner a gallon of wine and they sent me a heron roast, and after dinner I came and drank with them and took William Bretton with me, and

we had right good communication, and the person pleased me well as by the first communication.

She is young, little, and very well favoured and witty, and the country speaks much good by her. Sir, all this matter abiding the coming of her father to London, that we may understand what sum he will depart with, and how he likes me. He will be here within three weeks. I pray send me a letter how you think by this matter.

Sir, they have begun to ship at London, and all our wool and fell is yet in Cotswold, save four sarpliers; therefore we can do nothing at this time. Sir, I think money will be good at this market, for the King has sent to the merchants and let them wit [*know*] that he will have three whystyllys [*money changers' offices*]; one at Bruges, another at Calais, the third at London.

And as I am informed, what merchant of the Staple that sells his wool, he may buy what ware that he will again. And they that buy no ware shall bring in their money into

Owlpen Manor

Northleach

the King's whystyll at Bruges or Calais, and be paid at London at a month day, and the money shall be established at 8s. The merchants be not content therewith.

This lengthy letter gives us a glimpse of life in the Cotswolds at the time when their commercial importance was at its zenith. In medieval times much of the country's prosperity was founded on its wool trade with the Continent, and the Cotswolds were the powerhouse of this vast industry. Only Herefordshire wool commanded a higher price than that of the Cotswold Lions, but it was the Cotswolds that produced in bulk.

In Europe the best wool is English.
In England the best wool is Cotswold,

was the proud boast.

The land was largely owned by monastic houses, and to the wealthy abbots sheep were more important than men. The very church in which Richard Cely said matins, St Peter and St Paul in Northleach, was almost entirely rebuilt in the fifteenth century, so that it was virtually new in Cely's time, and he would have known it much as we do today.

WILLIAM MIDWINTER
AND WIFE, 1501

Perhaps most fascinating of all is the fact that one of the finest brasses in Northleach Church commemorates good old William Midwinter, who died in 1501. The image of him is rather sombre. He reclines with his hands clasped in prayer beside his wife Agnes, their four children kneeling below, and round the edge of the brass he bids his friends a dignified and pious farewell. How much happier to think of him as the local Mr Fixit who sets out to impress the cosmopolitan Cely by finding him a pretty girl in church.

The wealth of the monastic houses and merchants like Midwinter have left an indelible mark on Cotswold architecture, and the fine churches at Northleach, Chipping Campden, Fairford, Winchcombe and Cirencester are just a few of many surviving monuments to the trade.

As is explained, sarpliers, blottys and pokes were all sizes of sacks – and if you bought a pig in a poke, you could not see what you were getting. If Richard Cely had gathered in one trip 28 sarpliers of wool at 728lb, that represents nearly ten metric tonnes – and he was only one of many merchants buying on Cotteswold. Each of his sarpliers would have been one 'woolpack' to be sent by packhorse to London – 28 horses carrying, according to Cely, some 7,000 fleeces.

'The men of Pettit' refers to officers of John Petite, appointed by the Crown to make a search throughout the realm for defective wool and cheating by 'inwinding', the illegal practice of winding inferior wool among the locks of good fleeces. It was apparently especially prevalent in Dursley, which resulted in the phrase 'A Man of Dursley' for a cheat. Both John Smith (1619) and Daniel Defoe (1727) remark on it, and it was apparently in common usage throughout England from the sixteenth to the eighteenth century.

The reference to Thomas Limrick's sitting at Northleach for the King reflects the fact that he was a local Justice of the Peace as well as a Member of Parliament. His daughter about whom there was so much fuss was called Elizabeth.

The only other confusing phrase is '. . . and the money shall be established at 8s.' This refers to the rate of exchange, the

Flemish value of 8s. being the rate of exchange for one English angel (6s. 4d.) as set by the Crown. This was obviously a grumble from the merchants, who thought the canny Edward IV was trying to put one over on them.

Moving to the reign of Henry VIII we have the ITINERARY OF JOHN LELAND, written some time between 1535 and 1543. Leland made several trips through Gloucestershire and the Cotswolds, and these are a few excerpts from his various memoranda. They begin with his visit to Lechlade, entering the town from the Faringdon direction over St John's Bridge.

From Farington onto S. John's-bridge of 3. arches of stone and a causey a 3. miles *dim.* al by low grownd, and subject to the overflowinges of Isis.

As I rode over Isis I lernid that *Ulter. ripa* was in Glocestreshir, and *citerior* in Barkshir and Oxfordshir not far of.

I lernid that Northlech-broke, that cummith after to Estleche, enterith into Isis a litle byneth S. John's-bridge.

This Northlech water cummith from north to south.

Northlech is a praty uplandisch toune viij. miles from S. John's-bridge by north. Estleche is a 5. miles lower, both set *ripa citer.* as I cam.

At the very ende of S. John's-bridge *in ripa ulteriori* on the right hond I saw a chapelle in a medow, and greate enclosures of stone waulles.

From S. John's-bridge to Lechelade about half a mile. It is a praty olde village, and hath a pratie pyramis of stone, at the west ende of the chirch.

From Lechelade to Fairford about a 4. miles al by low ground, in a mer in a levelle, most apt for grasse, but very barein of wodde.

Fairford is a praty uplandisch toune, and much of it longith with the personage to Tewkesbyri-Abbay.

There is a fair mansion place of the Tames hard by the chirch yarde, buildid thoroughly by John Tame and

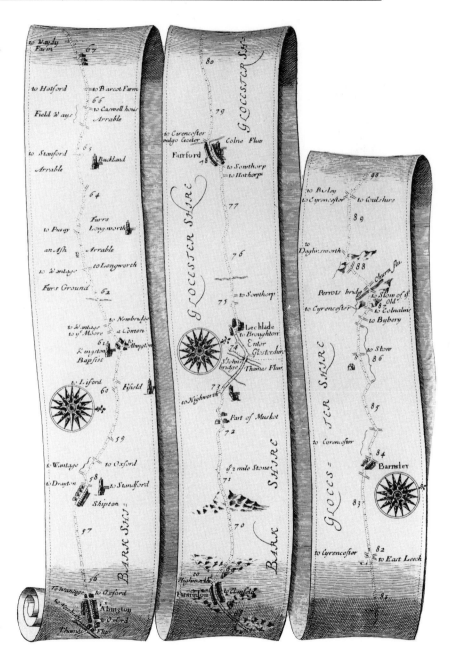

Batsford

Harescombe

Edmund Tame. The bakside whereof goith to the very bridg of Fairford.

Fairford never florishid afore the cumming of the Tames onto it.

John Tame began the fair new chirch of Fairforde, and Edmund Tame finishid it.

Going out of Fairford I passed over the water, wher is a bridg of 4. stone arches.

Ther cummith a litle bek by Pulton, that after goit at a mille a litle aboe Dounamney village into Amney water into the Isis.

From Pulton toward Amney villag I passid over Amney water, and so to Amney village, leving it on the right hand.

Amney brook risith a litle above Amney toune by north out of a rok: and goith a 3. miles of or more to Doune-amney wher Syr Antony Hungreford hath a fair house of stone.

Amney goith into Isis a mile beneth Dounamney again Nunne Eiton in Wilshir.

From Pulton to Cirencestre a 4. miles.

Cirencestre stondith on Churne ryver.

Churncestre callid in *Latine Corinium*.

There was afore the Conquest a fair and riche college of prebendaries in this toune; but of what Saxon's foundation no man can telle.

Henry the first made this college an abbay of chanons regulares, gyving them the landes of the prebendaries totally, and sum other thinges. Rumbaldas, chauncelar to King Edward the Confessor, was dene of this house, and buried in the body of the chirch, as it apperith by the epitaphy on his tumbe.

The est parte of the chirche of Cirencestre-Abbay shewith to be of a very old building. The west part from the *transeptum* is but new work to speke of. King Richard the first gave to Cirencestre the cortes and perquisites of 7. hundredes therabout yn Glocestreshir.

There hath bene 3. paroche chirchis in Cirencestre, whereof S. Cecilia chirch is clene doun, it was of late but a chapelle. S. Laurence yet stondith, but as no paroch chirch. There be 2. poor almose women endowid with landes.

There is now but one paroche chirch in al Cirencestre: but that is very fair.

The body of the chirch is al new work, to the which Ruthal, Bisshop of Duresme, borne and brought up in Cirencestre, promisied much, but preventid with deth gave nothing.

One Alice Aveling, aunt to Bisshop Ruthal by the mother side, gave a hundreth markes to the building of the right goodly porch of the paroch chirch.

Cirencestre is in Coteswolde.

Cirencestre hath the most celebrate market in al that quarters on Monday.

Tetbyri is vij miles from Malmesbyri, and is a praty market toun.

Tetbyri liyth a 2. miles on the lift hand from Fosse as men ryde to Sodbyri.

The hed of Isis in Coteswalde risith about a mile a this side Tetbyri.

The Fosse way goith oute at Cirencestre, and so streatchith by a manifest great creste to Sodbyri market . . . . miles of, and so to Bristow.

From Cirencestre to Malmesbyri viij miles.

First I roode about a mile on Fosse, then I turnid on the lifte hand, and cam al by champayne grounde, fruteful of corne and grasse, but very litle wood.

I passid over a stone bridg, wher as Newton water, as I tooke it, rennith in the very botom by the town, and so enterid into the toune by the este gate.

The toune of Malmesbyri stondith on the very toppe of a greate slaty rok, and ys wonderfully defendid by nature, for Newton water cummith a 2. miles from north to the toun: and Avon water cummith by weste of the toun from

Lokington village a 4. miles of, and meate aboute a bridg at south est part of the toun, and so goith Avon by south a while, and than turneth flat west toward Bristow.

The tounes men a late bought this chirch of the king, and hath made it their paroche chirch.

The body of the old paroch chirch, standing in the west end of the chirch yarde, is clene taken down.

Malmesbyri hath a good quik market kept every Saturday.

There is a right fair and costely peace of worke in the market place made al of stone and curiously voultid for poore market folkes to stande dry when rayne cummith.

Ther be 8. great pillers and 8 open arches: and the work is 8. square: one great piller in the midle berith up the voulte. The men of the toun made this peace of work *in hominum memoria*.

The hole logginges of the abbay be now longging to one Stumpe, an exceding riche clothiar that boute them of the king.

This Stumpes sunne hath maried Sir Edward Baynton's doughter.

This Stumpe was the chef causer and contributor to have the abbay chirch made a paroch chirch.

At this present tyme every corner of the vaste houses of office that belongid to the abbay be fulle of lumbes to weve clooth yn, and this Stumpe entendith to make a stret or 2. for clothiar in the bak vacant ground of the abbay that is withyn the toune waulles.

There be made now every yere in the toune a 3000 clothes.

Leland was obviously very impressed by Malmesbury, where the octagonal fifteenth-century market cross is still instantly recognisable from his description.

Also in Malmesbury, it is fascinating to note that within five years of the Dissolution of the Monasteries most of the religious buildings in the town had looms in them. This was the changeover era, from exporting wool to producing finished cloth. Leland was Keeper of the King's Libraries, and although he was ordained as a priest and a devoted antiquary, he does not seem to have had any sympathy for the suppressed monastic houses.

It is interesting that he renders Ampney as Amney, which is still the local pronunciation, and that Bristol is Bristow, the spelling before that peculiarity of the local accent that makes Maria Callas an 'operal singel' made its mark on the city's very name.

William Cobbett had some further thoughts on Malmesbury some 280 years later, to which we shall return.

Another of Leland's journeys touched the south-western escarpments of the Cotswolds, and these were his notes on Wotton-under-Edge and Dursley.

From Kynges Woode to Wotton a praty market towne, welle ocupyed withe clothiars havynge one fair long strete and welle buyldyd in it: and it stondithe clyvinge toward the rotes of an hill.

There be ruines of an olde maner place at Wotton by the paroche churche. It longgyd ons to the Berkeleys, and aftar onto the Lords Lisle. Syns forceable recoveryd of the Lord Berkeley her by sleinge the Lord Lisle.

Thens a 2. myles and more by very hilly and woddy ground to Doursley, where is a praty clothinge towne stoninge on a pece of the clyvinge of a hill, privilegid a 9. yers sens with a market. There is in the towne selfe a goodly springe, and is as the principall hedd of the broke servynge the tukkyng miles about the towne. This watar resortythe into Severne that is a boute 4. myles of towchinge by the way sume othar vilagis. This towne had a castle in it sumtyme longinge to the Berkeleys, syns to the Wiks, sens fell to decay, and is cleane taken downe. It had a metly good dyche about it, and was for the moste parte made of towfe stone full of pores and holes lyke a pumice. There is a quary of this stone about Dursley. Yt will last very longe.

Ludgate Hill, Wotton-under-Edge

High Street, Wotton-under-Edge

Dursley Castle was demolished shortly before Leland's visit, and much of the tufa stone was taken to Dodington, where it was used to build Dodington Park in around 1560. This house was replaced by a grander mansion in 1764, and the tufa then found its way into walls around the park.

Another of Leland's itineraries begins in Evesham:

From Eovesham I passyd a 6. or 7. miles all by champaine grownd in the Vale of Eovashame, being al or moste parte in Worchestar-shire, to Stanway-village, standynge in the rotes of the hills caullyd Coteswolde.

The vale of Eovesham is as it were for suche an angle the *horreum* of Wurcester-shire, it is so plentifull of corne. It lyethe from the left ripe of Avon to the very roots of Coteswolde-hilles.

There is in Stanway a fayre manor place and lordshipe, at the east ende of the churche, a late longing to the abbay of Tweukesbyri, where he some tyme lay. Mr. Tracy hathe it now in ferme.

There comithe downe from est-southe-est a broke that aftar goithe to Toddington streame.

From Stanway a mile to Dydbroke, and a quarter of a mile beyond is Hayles. There cummithe downe a prile of watar from the sowthe syde of Hayles abbay and goithe toward Todington water.

Frome Hailes to Winchelescombe a mile and halfe by fayre plentifull hills. The towne of Winchelescombe stand-ithe from a litle valley by est, and so softely risethe in lengthe of one principall streate into the west. The towne of certente, as it apperithe in divars places, and especially by south toward Sudeley-castle, was waullyd; and the legend, or lyfe of St. Kenelme doothe testifie the same.

There was a forteres or castelle right again the southe syde of St. Peter's. The paroche churche of Winchelescombe, caullyd of latar dayes (as apperithe by writyngs in Winchelescombe abbay) Ivy-castelle, now a place where a fewe poore housys be and gardines. I thinke that the old

buildings of it faullynge into ruine, and yvie growynge on the waulls of it, causyd [*it to be given*] the name of Ive-castle.

From Winchelescombe to Southam a 3 miles by good corne, pasture, and wood but somwhat hilly. Here dwelli-the Ser John Hudelstan, and hathe buyldyd a pratye maner place. He bought the land of one Goodman.

To Chiltenham, a longe toune havynge a market, a 4 or 5 miles. It longid to the abbay of Tewkesbyry, now to the kyng. A broke in the southe syd of the towne.

From Chiltenham to Glocestar a 6. miles all by low grounde, corne, pasture and medow. All the quartars there-about from Winchelescombe to Eovesham and to Twekes-byry, and all the way from Chiltenham to Glocestar, and thens to Twekesbery, and partly downe from Glocestar on Severne ripes to Newenham muche low grownd, subjecte to al sodeyne rysinges of Syverne: so that after reignes it is very foule to travayle in. I passyd over 2. or 3. smale bekks goinge betwixt Chiltenham and Glocestar, and they resorte to Severne.

The towne of Gloucestar is auncient, well buildyd of tymbar, and large, and strongly defendyd with waulls, wher it is not fortified with a depe streame of Severne watar. In the waull be 4. gates by este, west, northe and southe, and soe bere the names, but that the est-gate is commonly caullyd Aillesgate.

The auncient castle stondinge southe on the towne by Severne lefte ripe. The key on Severn lyfte ripe, whithar picards and small shippis cum, is almost by the castle. I learnyd there that the old key on Severne stode hard by St. Oswaldes, and for strife betwixt the towne and the howse of St. Oswald it was thens remevyd.

When the key was by St. Oswalds, there were divers praty streates that now be cleane decayed, as St. Bride's Strete and Sylver Gerdle Strete. The trothe is thos streats stod not moste holsomly, and were subject to the raginge flode of Severn, therefore men desired more to inhabite in

the higher places of the toun. The beautie of the towne lyeth in too crossing stretes, as the gates of the towne ly; and at the place of the midle metynge, or quaterfors of thes stretes, is aquaduklyd incastellid.

There be suburbes without the est, north, and south gates of Glocestar. The bridge only withe the causey lyethe at the west gate. The bridge that is on the chefe arme of Severne, that renethe hard by the towne is of 7. great arches of stone. There is anothar a litle more west of it, that hathe an arche or 2, and servythe at a tyme for a diche or dreane of the meads.

A litle way farthar is anothar bridge, hard witheout the weste gate, and this bridge hathe 5. greate archis. From this bridge there goithe a great causey of stone, forcyd up thrughe the low meds of Severn by the lengthe of a quartar of a myle. In this cawsey be dyvers doble arched bridges, to drene the medows at flods. At the end of this causey is a bridge of 8. arches not yet finished.

A prile of water is a bubbling brook, ripes are the banks of rivers and a picard is a small coastal or river vessel powered by sail, no doubt serving a similar purpose to the later Severn trows. The splendid 'aquaduklyd incastellid' at Gloucester Cross was some sort of gothic structure housing a water conduit.

It is perhaps surprising that, so soon after the Dissolution, Leland makes no mention of the Blood of Hailes, the notorious fake relic of Christ that brought pilgrims flooding to the abbey in medieval times. He does, however, allude to the weird legend of St Kenelm, the ninth-century prince of Mercia whose father Kenulf had made Winchcombe his capital.

After the king's death the story has it that the boy was murdered by his sister and buried under a thorn bush in Worcestershire – only for a white dove to issue from his body and bear news of the dastardly deed to the Pope in Rome. Word came from the Pontiff to have the child buried close to his father at Winchcombe Abbey, and on the night before the monks bearing the body reached the town, they rested on Sudeley Hill. A healing spring gushed up where they laid the coffin, and St Kenelm's Well remains a sight of Winchcombe to this day.

After the rabbit shoot

Deer and a cold Cotswold morning

For the next image it would have been welcome to have had a few words of praise from the Bard, but alas it is not to be. Although Shakespeare was born barely twenty miles from the hills, they appear but briefly in his works.

There is considerable evidence that Shakespeare had relations in Dursley, and possibly spent some of his time during his 'lost years' of 1583–92 in the suburb of Woodmancote, about half a mile south of the town centre. Legend has it that Shakespeare was prosecuted for deer-stealing by Sir Thomas Lucy of Charlecote Park, near Stratford, and it may have been while on the run that he took refuge here.

In HENRY IV, PART II and THE MERRY WIVES OF WINDSOR, which more or less followed one another, he has fun with one 'Justice Shallow' of Gloucestershire. Historians believe Shallow was a caricature of Lucy, his change of address being merely a reflection of Shakespeare's temporary interest in Gloucestershire.

Henry IV, Part II Act V Scene I

A Hall in Shallow's House

Davy (a servant of Shallow). I beseech you, sir, to countenance William Visor of Wincot against Clement Perkes of the hill.
Shallow. There are many complaints, Davy, against that Visor: that Visor is an arrant knave, on my knowledge.

The Merry Wives of Windsor

Shallow. Sir Hugh, persuade me not; I will make a Star-chamber matter of it; if he were twenty Sir John Falstaffs he shall not abuse Robert Shallow, esquire.
Slender (cousin to Shallow). In the county of Gloster, justice of peace, and *coram*.
Shallow. Ay, cousin Slender, and *Custalorum*.
Slender. Ay, and *Ratolorum too*; and a gentleman born, master parson; who writes himself *Armigero*; in any bill,

warrant, quittance or obligation – *Armigero!*
Shallow. Ay, that we do; and have done any time these three hundred years.
Slender. All his successors, gone before him, have done't; and all his ancestors, that come after him, may; they may give the dozen white luces in their coat.
Shallow. It is an old coat.
Evans (a Welsh parson). The dozen white louses do become an old coat well; it agrees well, passant: it is a familiar beast to man, and signifies – love.

Justice Shallow had come to Windsor from Gloucestershire to make a Star Chamber matter out of a poaching raid on his estate. The 'three luces hauriant argent' were the arms of the Charlecote Lucys! In both plays Shallow is the butt for Shakespeare's humour.

In the brief extract from Henry IV *Wincot is supposedly a reference to Woodmancote, and Visor a play on Vizard, a well-known Dursley family. The hill was presumably Stinchcombe, where a family by the name of Purchase – Perkes – lived in the sixteenth century.*

Another and better known passage involving the Cotswolds is to be found in Richard II, Scene III – The Wilds in Glostershire.

Bolingbroke. How far is it, my lord, to Berkley now?
North. Believe me, noble lord,
I am a stranger here in Glostershire:
These high wild hills and rough uneven ways
Draw out our miles, and make them wearisome;
And yet your fair discourse hath been as sugar,
Making the hard way sweet and delectable.
But I bethink me what a weary way
From Ravensburg to Cotswold will be found . . .

From these Cotswold connections we move on to firmer ground with John Smith or Smyth, a contemporary of Shakespeare although much longer-lived. He was born in 1567, three years after the Bard, but lived until 1641. Brought up in the Berkeley family, he became a barrister and was for many years steward of the hundred of Berkeley.

His three famous manuscripts are MEN AND ARMOUR FOR GLOUCESTERSHIRE IN 1608, THE LIVES OF THE BERKELEYS *and* THE HISTORY OF THE HUNDRED OF BERKELEY. *The purpose of the first was simply as a muster roll for the county; his master Henry, Lord Berkeley, was Lord Lieutenant at the time. It contains the names of all the 'able and sufficient men in body fit for His Majesty's service in wars, within the county of Gloucester', so covers most of the Cotswolds. It gives an indication of levels of population since in theory it lists all men aged between sixteen and sixty, giving their occupation and approximate age – 'about twenty', 'about forty', 'between fifty and three score'.*

It tells whether he is 'of the tallest stature, fit to make a pikeman', 'of a middle stature, fit to make a musketeer' or 'of a lower stature, fit to serve with a caliver [light musket]'. Then there were inevitably those 'of the meanest stature, either fit for a pioneer or of little other use'.

The levels of population and occupations are interesting; the southern Cotswolds are predominantly weavers, tuckers and clothiers, all trades associated with the woollen industry. In the parish of Owlpen, near Uley, of seventeen men listed, thirteen are weavers, one is a fuller, one a tailor and the other two are labourers. In other words, seventy-six per cent of the male workforce is associated with the woollen industry.

Although not all parishes would have been similar, the industry was the major source of employment for a wide belt of the south-western Cotswolds including all of the Stroud, Dursley and Wotton valleys. On the northern Cotswolds, the landscape is totally different and the water power for the mills was not so readily available. Here the occupations cover a wide variety, but the largest category is that of labourer. Because of the woollen industry, the south-western parishes had a much higher level of

population, and when the industry collapsed at the beginning of the nineteenth century there was distressing hardship.

To give a flavour of Smith's muster roll, this is a small section from the entry for Chipping Campden:

> John Boulter sheppeard. 3. ca.
> Avery Harris wever. 2. m.
> ffrancis Heynes laborer.
> ffrancis Ward. 2. p. tr.
> Edward Ruell mason. 2. ca.
> Christofer Blackly Tanner. 2. p.
> Richard Poynter laborer. 2. ca.
> William Addams husbandman. 2. ca.
> John Harrys Taylor. 2. ca.
> John Knedon Collermaker. 1. ca.
> Roger Rawlins laborer. 2. m.
> John Wiggen laborer.
> Thomas Bate husbandman. 3. ca.
> Henry Wyttone laborer. 2. py.

Poor Henry Wyttone, 'about forty' and of the meanest stature, was ready-made to be a pioneer – or of little other use . . .

It is unfortunate that in his more anecdotal works Smith did not cover a larger area than the hundred of Berkeley, as he cannot resist telling a good tale. One describes how the wicked Earl Godwin acquired the Berkeley lands from poor innocent nuns in the year 1043, some twenty-three years before the Norman Conquest.

Berkeley neere unto Severne is a towne of £500 revenue; in it there was a nunnery, and the abbesse over theis nunnes was a noble woman and beautifull: Earl Goodwyn, by a cunninge and subtile witt desiringe not her selfe but hers, as hee passed that way, leaft with her a nephew of his, a very proper and beautifull yonge gentleman, (pretending that hee was sickely) untill he returned backe.

Berkeley Castle

Bagendon

Him hee had given this lesson, that hee shoulde keepe his bed, and in no wise seeme to bee recovered, untill hee had got both her, and as many of the Nunnes as hee could, with child, as they came to visit him: and to the end the yonge man might obteine their favour and his full purpose when they visited him, the Earle gave unto him pretty rings and fine girdles to bestow for favours upon them, and therby to deceive them.

Hee therfore beinge gladly and willingly entred into this course of libidinous pleasure, (for that way downe to hell is easy), was taught his lessons, and wisely playeth the foole in that which seemed wise in his own conceit: with him were restant all those thinges which the foolish virgins could wish for, beauty, dainty delicates, ritches, faire speach; and carefull hee was nowe to single them alone; the Devil therfore thrust out Pallas, brought in Venus, and made the church of our Saviour and his saints an accursed temple of all idolls, and the shrine a very stewes.

And so of pure lambes hee made them foule shee wolves, and of pure virgins filthy harlots; now when as many of their bellies bare out bigge and round, this youth beinge by this time over-wearied with conquest of pleasure, getteth him gone, and forthwith bringeth home unto his lord and maister a victorious ensigne, worthy to have the reward of iniquity, and to speake plainly, relateth what was done.

Noe sooner heard hee this, but hee hieth him to the kinge, informeth him how the lady Abbesse of Berkeley and her Nunnes were great with childe, and commonly prostitute to every one that would, sendeth messengers on purpose for enquiry therof, proveth all that hee had said; hee beggeth Berkeley of the kinge his lord, after the Nunnes were thrust out, and obtaineth it at his hands . . .

In the same manuscript, which Smith appears to have completed in 1639, he describes a popular pastime on the Cotswolds . . .

The large and levell playnes of Slimbridge warth and others in the vale of this hundred: and the downes or hilly playnes of Stintescombe, Westridge, Tickruydonge and others in the hilly or Cotteswold part, doe witnes the inbred delight that both gentry, yeomanry, rascallity, boyes and children doe take in a game called Stoball, the play whereat each child of 12 years old, can I suppose as well describe as my selfe. And not a sonne of mine but at 7 was furnished with his double stoball staves, and a gamster thereafter.

Unfortunately Smith presumes that everyone knows about Stoball, and therefore declines to describe how it is played. THE OXFORD ENGLISH DICTIONARY *is of little help, suggesting it was similar to golf, but with 'double stoball staves' perhaps it was more akin to cricket. John Aubrey in his* NATURAL HISTORY OF WILTSHIRE *of 1686 is a little more helpful . . .*

Stobball-play is peculiar to North Wilts, North Gloucestershire, and a little part of Somerset near Bath. They smite a ball, stuffed very hard with quills and covered with soale leather, with a staffe, commonly made of withy, about 3 [*feet*] and a halfe long . . . A Stobball ball is of about four inches diameter, and as hard as stone.

The vital information he omits is whether the ball is stationary when it is smitten!
But back to Smith and Berkeley country:

In the body of this hundred are observed three steps or degrees, obvious to every observer: The first from the chanell of Severne halfe way towards the hills, which hath wealth without health. The second, from thence neere towards the tops of those hills, which hath wealth and health. And the third steppe or degree, from thence forward called the weald or Cotsall part, affordeth health in that sharpe air but lesse wealth, and seemes to take name of the barren wooddy parts. Into the best wherof the mercifull goodnes of almighty God hath cast my lott, beyond my hopes or desires.

Smith, who lived in North Nibley, seems here to be giving evidence for the wealth of the woollen industry on the Cotswold escarpment and valley sides.

He devotes several pages to how the working people of Gloucestershire spoke in the early seventeenth century, along with some local proverbs and sayings. Many of these characteristics live on to this day in some rural areas, in spite of the fact that the BBC has been bringing standard English into our homes for sixty years or more. 'Her' for 'she' and phrases like 'putton up' for 'put it up' are still in common everyday use, though it has to be said that they are more favoured by the older generation.

Smith then lists 100 proverbs, many of which are difficult to understand. These are among the less cryptic:

1. Hee's like an Aprill shoure, that wets the stone 9 times in an houre. Hee's like a feather on an hill. — Applyed to an unconstant man.

3. Hee'l proove, I thinke, a man of Durseley. i.e. A Man that will promise much but performe nothinge. This (now dispersed over England), tooke roote from one Webb, a great Clothier dwellinge in Durseley in the daies of Queen Mary, as also was his father in the time of Kinge Henry the viijth, usinge to buy very great quantities of wooll out of most counties of England.

At the waighinge wherof, both father and sonne, (the better to drawe on their ends) would ever promise out of that parcell a gowncloth, peticote cloth, apron or the like to the good wife or her daughters, but never paid any thinge. Old Edward Greene, vicar of Berkeley in the first of Kinge James, usinge this proverbe in his sermon there whereat many of Dursley were present, had almost raised a tumult amongst his auditory, wherof my selfe was one.

4. Hee seekes for stubble in a fallowe feild, i.e. hee looseth his labour, Or as wee otherwise speake, seekes for a needle in a bottle of hay.

6. Hee that feares every grasse must never pisse in a meadow. In like sense as A faint hart never won a faire lady.

7. Hee that's cooled with an Apple and heated with an egge, Over mee shall never spread his legg. — A widowe's wanton proverbe.

8. Neighbour, w'are sure of faire weather, each ha behelde this morne Abergainy hill [*the Sugar Loaf, near Abergavenny*]. — A frequent speach with us of the hilly part of this hundred and indeed, that little picked hill in Wales over that Towne is a good Alminake maker; wherof my selfe have often made use in my husbandry.

9. Hee is very good at a white pott. — By white pot, wee westerners doe meane a great custard or puddinge baked in a bagg, platter, kettle, or pan: notinge heerby, a good trencher man, or great eater.

11. A great houskeeper is sure of nothinge for his good cheare, save a great Turd at his gate. I wish this durty proverbe had never prevailed in this hundred, havinge from thence banished the greater halfe of our ancient hospitallity.

12. My catt is a good moushunt. — An usuall speach when wee husbands commend the diligence of our wives. Wee hundreders maintaininge as an orthodox position that hee that somtimes flattereth not his wife cannot alwaies please her.

15. The gray mare is the better horse. — Meaninge that the most master goeth breechlesse: i.e. when the silly husband must aske his wife whether it shall bee a bargaine or not.

16. Money is noe foole, if a wise man have it in keepinge.

Dursley

Painswick

— Alluding to the old common sayinge, — That a foole and his money are soone parted.

17. When wheat lies longe in bed, it riseth with an heavy head. When wheat is sowne in October or November, and by reason of an heavy furrowe cast upon it or other accident of nyppinge wether shewes not above ground till December or January, Our plowmen say It will at harvest have the greater eare; But, (by the leave of my fellow ploughmen and theire proverbe), I thinke both they and my selfe bury neere halfe the seed wee sowe in that manner, that never riseth.

20. Hee mends like sowre ale in sommer. i.e. Hee growes from nought to worse.

21. Hee hath offered his candle to the divell. — This (now common) thus arose; Old ffillimore [*Phillimore*] of Cam, going in Anno 1584 to present Sir Thomas Throgmorton of Tortworth with a suger lofe, met by the way with his neighbour S M, who demanded whither and upon what business hee was goinge answered, 'To offer my candle to the Divill': which cominge to the eares of Sir Tho: At the next muster hee sent two of ffillimores sonnes soldiers into the low countries, where one was slayne and the other at a deere rate redeemed his returne.

22. Be-gis, Be-gis, it's but a man's fancy. — A frequent speach which thus arose: William Bower of Hurst Farme had each second yeare one or more of his maidservants with childe, whom, with such portions as hee bestowed upon them, hee maryed either to his menservants (perhaps also sharers with him), or to his neighbors' sonnes of meaner ranke.

Some yeares past, it was demaunded of A. Cl. why hee beinge of an estate in wealth well able to live would marry one of Bower's double whores (for by her hee had had two bastards), wherto A. Cl. soberly replyed: Begys, Begys, it's but a man's fancy, it's but a man's fancy: meaninge

take which of the constructions you please; In both senses it's common with us hundreders.

23. Gett him a wife, get him a wife. W. Quinten of Hill havinge a pestilent angry and unquiet wife, much more insultinge over his milde nature then Zantippe over Socrates, was oft enforced to shelter himselfe from those stormes, to keepe his chamber: whence, hearinge his neighbors complayninge of the unrulines of their towne bull, whom noe mounds would keepe out from spoilinge of their corne feilds, the bull then bellowing before them, and they in chasing him towards the common pound; peepinge out of his chamber windowe cryed to them; Neighbors, Neighbors, gett him a wife, gett him a wife; meaninge That by that meanes hee would bee made quiett and tamed as himselfe was: from whence this proverbe (nowe frequent) first arose.

24. If once againe I were Jack Tomson or John Tomson, I would never after bee good man Tomson while I lived: Hence this, thus: This Jacke Tomson, soe called till sixteene, and after John Tomson till hee maryed at 24, was the only jovyall and frolicke younge man at merry meet- ings and Maypoles in all Beverston, where hee dwelled: After his maryage, (humors at home not well settlinge betweene him and his wife), hee lost his mirth and began to droope, which one of his neighbors often observinge, demanded upon a fit opportunity, the cause of his bad cheare and heavy lookes.

Wherto, hee sighing gave this answere: Ah neighbor, if once againe I were either Jacke Tomson or John Tomson, I would never bee goodman Tomson while I lived: This story I derived from William Bower the elder, the olde Bayle of this hundred, upon whose kinsman the instance was; And from whome his owne case dissented but little.

30. Beware, Clubs are trumps; Or clubs will prove trumps. A caution for maids to be gone, for their Mis-

tress's anger hath armed her with a cudgell: Or, to the silly husband to bee packinge, for his wife draweth towards her altitude.

31. Hee's a true chipp of the old blocke. Like sonne like father.

32. All the maids in Wanswell may dance in an egg shell. I hold this a lying proverbe at this day, it slandereth some of my kindred that dwell there.

34. Simondsall sauce, usual to note a guest bringinge an hungry appetite to our table: Or when a man eates little, to say hee wants some Simondsall sauce: The farme of Simondsall stands on the highest place and purest aire of all that country: If any situation could promise long and healthy daies I would thence expect it: provided I have a good woodpile for winter.

35. Simondsall newes. The clothiers, horscarriers and wainsmen of this hundred who weekely frequent London, knowinge by ancient custome That the first question (after welcome home from London) is What newes at London; Doe usually gull us with feigned inventions, devised by them upon those downes; which wee either, then suspectinge upon the report or after findinge false, wee cry out, Simondsall newes. A general speach betweene each coblers teeth.

36. Hee is as milde as an hornett. Meaninge a very waspe in tongue or trade; This proverbe I have from my wife, a true Cowleian, and naturall bred hundredor; A proverb as frequent with her as chidinge with her maides.

41. An head that's white to mayds brings noe delight: or An head that's gray serves not for maydens play: In which state my constitucion now stands.

44. A man may love his house well though hee ride not upon the ridge: Or Love well his cowe though hee kisse her not.

49. If thou lov'st mee at the hart, thou'lt not loose mee for a fart. Often varied into divers applicacions.

51. Smoke will to the smicker: meaninge, If many gossips sit against a smokey chimney the smoke will bend to the fairest; A proverb which doth advantage a merry gossip to twitt the foule slutt her neighbour.

55. My milke is in the Cowes horne, now the zunne is 'ryv'd at Capricorne: meaninge, when the dayes are at shortest, the cowe commonly fed with strawe and neere calvinge gives little or no milk.

59. In descripcion of our choicest morsells, wee say; The backe of an hearinge, the poll of a tench, The side of a salmon, the belly of a wench.

62. As bawdy as a butcher: meaninge, that filthines stickes to his conditions as visibly as grease to the butcher's apron.

63. Hee that will thrive must rise at five; But hee that hath thriven may lye till seaven.

64. Hee that smells the first favour is the fault's first father. This proverb admits many applicacions: The homlyest is, That hee first smells the fart that lett it.

82. Things ne'ere goe ill where Jack and Gill pisse in one quill.

83. A woman, spaniell, and a walnut tree, The more they are beaten, better they bee.

84. Much smoke little fire; much adoe about nothinge.

93. Botch and fit, build and flit. I bethrew this proverbe, wherby the tenant is kept from a comly repairinge of his house for doubt of havinge it taken in revertion over his head.

Compton Abdale

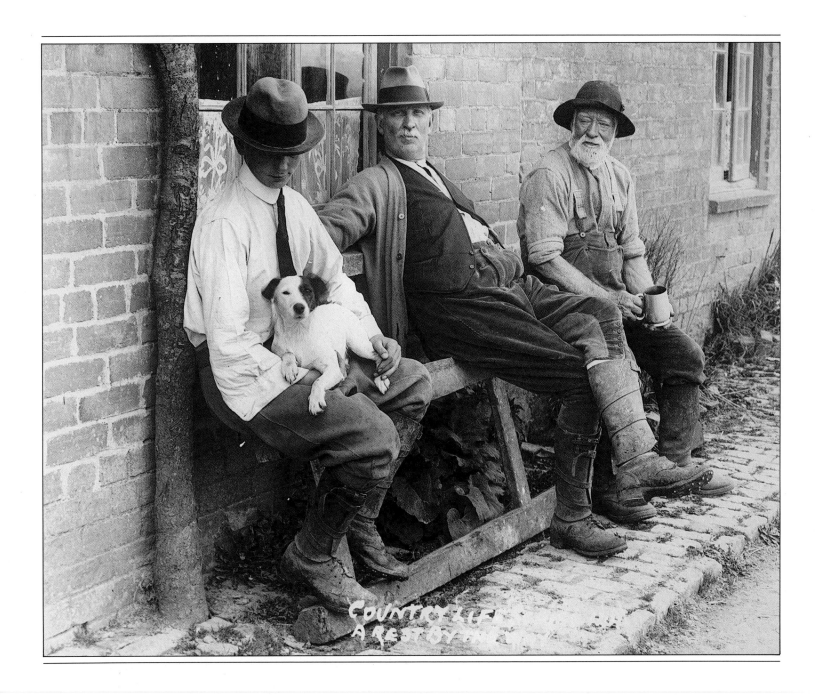

A rest by the way . . .

95. The mice will play when the catt is away. i.e. Servants will loyter when the master is absent: This my experience in my long abodes abroade, all my life longe, hath prooved too true for my profitt.

Smith was quite at home using the vernacular phrases of the common man; the prudish era was still more than 150 years away. One interesting proverb is number 17, where it would seem to imply that he was not averse to taking a hand at ploughing.

In his history of the hundred he makes some interesting comments on Puritan activity. He was writing in 1639, only a year before the start of the Civil War, and in references to Alkington and Stinchcombe he describes ancient amusements and annual customs such as the Whitsun Ales, stamped out by killjoys.

. . . Betweene the hambletts of Wike and Nuport is a little meade called Riam, whither on Sunday next after Whitsunday resorted the youthes of both sexes from many Villages adjoyninge, spendinge the afternoone in dancinge, leapinge, wrastlinge and the like exercises; a day knowne in all the quarters therabouts by the matronimicall name of Riam-mead sunday; A meetinge of late years omitted.

And for Stinchcombe:

. . . Heere in Stinchcombe is a parcel of ground called blu-meade; from whence wee hundredors in theis parts have amongst us the name of Blu-meade Sunday, the second Sunday after the feast of Pentecost; a Place where the younger sort of both sexes accustomed in the afternoon of that day to meete from the Townships adjoininge

to dance, leape, wrastle, and disport themselves till eveninge; of late yeares by some severe and rigid Catoes exclaiminge against such recreations, quite discontinued.

Leaping and wrastling were obviously common in the south Cotswolds as well as farther north near Chipping Campden, where Robert Dover held his 'Cotswold Olimpicks'. Smith was evidently not a Puritan, but in other ways he was reactionary as he commented with wistful regret on the freeing of the serfs, villeins and bondsmen . . .

In this Manor or Tithinge also, and in all or most of this Hundred, the lords therof have had divers villeins or bondservants imployed in the husbandries therof under the oversight of the Reeve of the Manor, who was their principall husbandman, untill the time of our last civill warres betweene the houses of Yorke and Lancaster.

Of whom I have seene many sales and grants by divers Deeds, some of whom continued till the end of Kinge Edward the fourth and the beginninge of Henry the viith, when the last manumission was by William lord Berkeley in this manor, that I have observed. And I conceive, that the lawes concerninge Villeinage are still in force, of which the latest are the sharpest; But now . . . since slaves were made free which were of great use and service, there are growne up a rabble of Rogues, cut purses and the like mischeivous men, slaves in nature though not in lawe.

What would Smith have made of the Levellers in Burford in 1649? Their brand of social democracy was far too much for Oliver Cromwell, and for Smith it would have been the beginning of the end of life as he knew it. Happily, he did not have to endure it, dying in 1641 at the age of seventy-five.

The Whitsun Ales of which the celebrations at Stinchcombe formed a part were widespread. The Randwick Mop or 'Runnick Wap', described by Rudder later, and enjoyed to this day in that hillside village above Stroud, is an exception in that it survived beyond its initial Puritan suppression.

In 1641, the zeal of 'that worthy Divine' Mr Henry Burton was celebrated in a publication entitled A DIVINE TRAGEDIE LATELY ACTED, OR A COLLECTION OF SUNDRIE MEMORABLE EXAMPLES OF GOD'S JUDGEMENTS UPON SABBATH-BREAKERS, AND OTHER LIKE LIBERTINES, IN THEIR UNLAWFULL SPORTS, HAPPENING WITHIN THE REALME OF ENGLAND In this pamphlet Mr Burton recorded with relish the mishaps that occurred at Whitsun Ales, all of which he put down to God's wrath.

A Miller at Churchdown, neer Glocester, [*in 1634*] would needs (contrary to the admonitions both of his Minister in private, and generally in publike, yea and that very day, and of other Christian friends) keep a solemn Whitson ale, for which he had made large preparation and provision, even of threescore dozen of cheesecakes, with other things proportionable, in the Church-house, half a mile from his Mill, his musicall instruments were set forth on the side of the Church-house, where the Minister and people were to passe to the Church to Evening Prayer.

When Prayer and Sermon were ended the Drumme is struck up, the peeces discharged, the Musicians play, and the rowt fall a dauncing till the evening; when they all with the Miller resort to his Mill; where that evening before they had supt, about nine of the clock on Whitsunday, a fire took suddenly in his house over their heads, and was so brief and quick that it burnt down his house and mill and devoured with all the greatest of all his other provisions and houshold-stuffe. This is confirmed by sundry good testimonies.

Upon May Eve [*1635*] Thomas Troe, of Glocester, Carpenter, in the parish of S. Michael, some coming unto him and asking him whether he would go with them to fetch the May-pole, he swore by the Lord's wounds that he would, though he never went more. Now whiles he was working on the May-pole on May day morning, before he had finished his work, the Lord smote him with such a lamenesse and swelling in all his limbs that he could neither go nor lift his hands to his mouth to feed himself, but kept his bed for half a yeer together, and stil goes lame to this day; May 4, 1636.

About a yeer since, 1636, in Ashton under the Hill, in the Parish of Beckford, in the county of Glocester, the Minister there, Mr. Blackwell, having occasion in his Sermon in the afternoon on the Lord's day to reprove the prophaning of that day by sports &c., as soon as the Sermon was done, a young man of that place used these words, 'Now Mr. Blackwell hath done, we'le begin'; and so taking the cudgels, playes with them; and at the second or third bout, he received a thrust in one of his eyes that thrust it quite out, so as it hanged by, and could never recover it again.

The most famous of the Whitsun Ales developed into the Cotswold Olimpick Games under Robert Dover, who was born in Norfolk in around 1582. He was educated at Cambridge and studied at the bar before moving to Gloucestershire in 1611. It was apparently at Whit week in 1612 that he was first involved in organising the games that still bear his name, but those early ventures were doubtless merely a continuation of the traditional Whitsun Ale. It was only later that his revels developed their distinctive style.

The games included horse racing, hare coursing, running, jumping, hammer-throwing, wrestling and quarter staff fencing. For gentler souls there were dancing contests, both mixed and for women alone, performed to the sound of bagpipe and drum; and in tents on the side of what is still known as Dover's Hill there were games of skill and chance.

In 1636 the Puritan minister William Bartholomew came to Chipping Campden making life difficult for Dover, who was sympathetic to Catholicism and clearly concerned about the growth of the Puritan movement.

Like the many poets who referred to the games as harmless,

Northleach

Tetbury

Dover was aware of the controversy over sports. He and the poets argued that activities such as running, leaping and dancing were to be encouraged and had royal approval – they kept men fit for the wars, and out of alehouses. Yet many Puritans believed there was an excessive addiction to games, and they were particularly down on anything that might lead to immorality, rowdiness and drunkenness, as well as festivals which had pagan origins or violated the Sabbath.

The Civil War, together with the likes of William Bartholomew, put a temporary end to the games, but the Restoration brought a revival and it was not until drunken hordes swooped down in force from the Midlands in Victorian times that a more lengthy halt was called. Now Dover's Games and their parallel Scuttlebrook Wake flourish once again.

The county historian Rudder said of the games in 1779:

Mr. Robert Dover, who lived in the reign of king J.I., instituted certain diversions on the Coteswold, called after his name, which were annually exhibited about Willersey and Campden. Even now there is something to be seen of

them, every Thursday in Whitsun-week, at a place about half a mile from Campden called Dover's Hill.

The Coteswold games and their patron are celebrated in a small collection of poems intituled *Annalia Dubrensia*, written by Michael Drayton, Ben. Johnson and about thirty other eminent persons of their time, mostly addrest to the patron of the games; by means of which, if you believe the poet,

> Cotswold, that barren was, and rough before,
> Is tempe now become, Cotswold no more.
> Pan may go pipe in barren Malvern chase;
> The fawns and Satyrs seek some other place.
> Cotswold is now th'epitome of myrth;
> And joy, presaged erst, is come to birth.
> Olympus' mount, that e'en to this day fills
> The world with fame, shall to thy Cotswold hills
> Give place and honour. Hercules was first
> Who those brave games begun: Thou, better nurst,
> Dost in our anniverse most nobly strive
> To do in one year what he did in five.

Bristol taking
Exeter shaking
Gloucester quaking . . .

So went the words of a Royalist rhyme in 1643, the year of the Civil War that saw most activity in Gloucestershire and the Cotswolds.

Generally the county had greater sympathy for the cause of Parliament and its Puritan bias, rather than for the party of the king. There were various reasons. West Gloucestershire, which was economically dependent on the Severn, saw the ship money tax for warships as an important local issue. In 1635 and 1640 the county produced only two per cent of the £5,500 demanded.

The north Cotswolds, especially the north-west around Winchcombe and Cheltenham, produced a great deal of tobacco, and the threat of Royalist Virginian tobacco was very real to the community.

One of the county's foremost recorders of the war was John Corbet, who was twenty-two in 1642. Born in Gloucester, he attended a local grammar school, was a bachelor of Magdalen College, Oxford, at sixteen, and by the time he was twenty he was back in his home city as incumbent at St Mary de Crypt. By the outbreak of the Civil War he was chaplain to the parliamentarian governor of Gloucester, Colonel Edward Massey.

Corbet wrote his account two years after the action. This passage, full of the flavour of the period, tells of Prince Rupert's capture of Cirencester before the Siege of Gloucester.

About the first of January 1643, the maine strength of the king's army came before Cirencester prepared and resolved to storme it, yet they only faced the towne, and after two daies were strangely taken off, either disabled by the extreame cold on the hills, or some suddaine misfortune, or daunted by the shew of unanimity and resolution in the people, or else clouded in their thoughts by the secret will of God in the nick of action, that they made not the least attempt, but threatned an afterclap.

A few daies after our forces had their designe upon Sudely castle, at that time kept by Captaine Bridges in the behalfe of the Lord Chandos. Lieutenant Colonell Massie was intrusted with the manage of this action, who drew from Gloucester a party of three hundred musketteers, with two sakres assisted with foure-score horse, and foure companies of dragoones from Cirencester by order of a counsell of warre held there, and consent of the deputy lieutenants.

There were in the castle neere threescore souldiers, with provision and ammunition sufficient: our men drew up before it in the evening, made severall shotts, and the canon did some execution; the same night summons was given, the enemy refused to render upon quarter, but craved time till the next day, which in part was granted; guards were set upon them all night, the next morning our men were drawne out to make an assault, beds and wooll-packs were fetched out of the neighbourhood, which they tumbled before, and saved themselves from shot.

The horse and dragoones came up before the foot approached the wall, and possest themselves of a garden under the castle, and got hay and straw which they fired, that the smoake driven by the wind smothered the house, in the shadow of which the ordnance were brought up undiscovered, and planted against the weakest part of the castle, which when the enemy perceived they sounded a parley, and immediately rendred upon agreement.

The conditions were that all might have liberty of person, and passe to their owne houses, leaving their armes behind, and taking an oath never to serve against the parliament: they compounded also for the goods in the house, for which they were to pay five hundred pounds within six daies, or to leave them a free prize to the souldiers.

Within two daies after Prince Rupert faced Sudely with about five thousand horse and foot pretending an attempt

Bringing home the orphan

Taynton

to regaine it, but in the meane time marched his artilery towards Cirencester. Lieutenant Colonell Massie made provision to maintaine the castle by taking in water, and store of hay and corne, and having left there Lieutenant Colonell Forbes with a sufficient guard, himselfe retreated to Gloucester; the prince with his force kept the hills, and after three daies fell before Cirencester, a stragling and open towne, neither well fortified nor capable of defence.

The champaine country round about was most advantagious to the horse, in which the enemies' strength did chiefly consist, and which was then wholly wanting to that garrison, for their horse and dragoones were sent to the taking of Sudely: most of their officers were drawne out upon that service except the captaines of the volunteers, and Lieutenant Colonell Karre was the only experienced souldier left there: their canoneers were wanting, the common souldiers quite off the hinges, either cowardly or mutinous.

The storme rose when least feared by the miserable people, who had not ended the joy of their late deliverance from as great a power but strangely diverted; and though they were still in the same danger upon the reverse of the army, yet were they not capable of the least distrust, till the storme hovered againe, either supposing themselves invincible, or by defiance bafled a wary enemy, that falls backe and waites his time to returne with greater fury.

On the second of February the towne was assaulted and taken; the first and maine assault was made on a house a flight shot from the town, which was defended by a hundred musketeers for an houre's space against two regiments of foot, and a regiment of horse which were led on by the prince, till at length having drawne up their musketeers, and by granadoes fired the barnes and ricks and smoothered the guard, the enemie's horse drove their foote before them, entred the streetes by maine force, and possest themselves of the garrison within two houres. Yet it cost them the lives of many, amongst whom the Welch-men were reported to suffer the greatest slaughter, who in that army were a continuall sacrifice to the sword.

Each guard made resistance according to the officers' valour and experience; the souldiers of the Earl of Stamford's regiment had acted the best part but that they were most put to the sword when the towne was entred, except those that by flight had their lives given them for a prey. Some few besides defended their guards a while, but the passages were many and open, and the enemy soone came upon their backes; as for the country-men, their houre was not yet come, neither had they quitted such imployment as did infeeble their spirits, not entred the schoole of war to study indignation, revenge and bloud, that alone can overcome the terrour of an army.

It so fell out that in the midst of the service they were at their wits end, and stood like men amazed, feare bereft them of understanding and memory, begat confusion in the minde within, and the thronging thoughts did oppresse and stop the course of action, that they were busied in everything, but could bring forth nothing; few of ours were slaine in the fight, but many murthered after the taking of the towne. . . The whole country was quickly full of this disaster, and in vaine did thinke to recover what was lost by weaknesse of spirit or errour in the chief manage of the businesse; thousands of men armed and unarmed flocked together, and resolved to undertake the enemy under the conduct of a grave and well-minded patriot. . .

The very next day after the loss of Cirencester the city of Gloucester was demanded by Prince Rupert, the summons found the people extreamely dashed at the strange turn of things, and so much amazed that they could not credit the report of this blow, though confirmed by sundry eye-witnesses; the hearts of many sunke very low and began to lye flat, zeale and religion upheld some, all had a kinde of will; but the strong fidelity and resolution of the souldier at that time, and in all extreame hazards, upheld the garrison.

Corbet obviously witnessed much of this action at first hand, for how else could he have come up with such a classic description of men at war as:

They were at their wits end, and stood like men amazed, feare bereft them of understanding and memory, begat confusion in the minde within, and the thronging thoughts did oppresse and stop the course of action. . .

For five and a half months the city remained safely held for parliament, although all around, the country was falling to the king. The surrender of Bristol on 26 July, 1643 was particularly demoralising for the men holding Gloucester. On 6 August a small Roundhead party left the Northgate and took ten Cavaliers prisoner at Wotton-under-Edge, returning north via Painswick. There they spotted enemy cavalry, and on 10 August the king himself arrived at the outskirts of Gloucester, with a force that was soon to rise to 30,000 men.
 This was the message he sent the city:

Charles Rex

Out of our tender compassion to our city of Gloucester, and that it may not receive prejudice by our army, which we cannot prevent if we be compelled to assault it: we are personally come before it, to require the same, and are graciously pleased to let all the inhabitants of, and all other persons within that city, as well souldiers as others, know that if they shall immediately submit themselves, and deliver this city to us, we are contented freely and absolutely to pardon every one of them without exception, and doe assure them in the word of a king, that they nor any of them shall receive the least dammage or prejudice by our army in their persons, or estates. But that we will appoint such a governor, and a moderate garrison to reside there as shall both for the ease and security of that city, and the whole county.

Antient Gloucester..
From Speed's Map, Publifhed 1610.
The Fortifications are from Hall & Pinnells Map.
Lithographic Press, 10, King Street, Weſtʳ

But if they shall neglect this offer of grace, and favour, and compell us by the power of our army to reduce that place (which by the helpe of God we shall easily and shortly be able to doe) they must thanke themselves for all the calamities, and miseries that shall befall them. To this message we expect a cleare and positive answer within two houres after the publishing hereof, and by these presents doe give leave to any persons safely to repaire to, and returne from us, whom that city shall desire to imploy unto us in that businesse, and we do require all the officers and souldiers of our army, quietly to suffer them to passe accordingly.

Little Wolford

Painswick

Corbet takes up the story again:

The king by this time drew into the field before the towne, attended by Prince Charles, the Duke of Yorke, Prince Rupert, and General Ruthen, faced us with about six thousand horse and foote on that side, and two thousand horse on the other side. After some debate upon the message, an answer was drawn, consented unto, both by citizens and souldiers, and presented to his majesty by Serjeant Major Pudsey and a citizen:

'We the inhabitants, magistrates, officers and souldiers within this garrison of Gloucester, unto his majestie's gratious message return this humble answer, that we do keep this city according to our oath and allegiance, to and for the use of his majesty and his royall posterity, and doe accordingly conceive our selves wholly bound to obey the commands of his majesty signified by both houses of parliament; and are resolved by God's help to keep this city accordingly.'

For two weeks the king's huge force could do little more than sit and wait through daily rounds of cannon fire and small skirmishes. The city casualties during this period were very few, but among them were a boy and girl who peeped over the city wall, and a pig killed by a cannon ball which had landed harmlessly and was simply rolling down a street. About this time the king threatened to hang the twelve city aldermen from the twelve city inn signs, and on 24 August he sent in two lawyers from Tewkesbury with a further request for surrender. This received a negative reply, and was celebrated in verse:*

> Two pettifogging lawyers came of late
> In love to tell us of our present state . . .
> (our answer) But for your bug-beare threats so huge and big,
> If seven score cannons can but kill one pig . . .
> All know full well
> That every Bell
> Is useless till't be hanged;
> And none I hope
> Denies a rope
> To have his sides well banged.

The surrounding armies' tactics included attempts to mine under the city walls and assaults by siege engines. Local legend even holds that the failure of the latter gave rise to the nursery rhyme Humpty Dumpty, but it is a mistaken belief. There are versions of the Humpty Dumpty rhyme to be found all over Europe. Humpty is Lille Trille in Denmark, Gigele-Gagele in Germany, Boule-Boule in France and Annebadadeli in Switzerland. The Royalists had a Roman-style siege engine built for them by one Dr. Chillingworth, but when this was pushed up to the wall, it was successfully toppled and smashed by the defenders. It was presumably this action which caused the delighted parliamentarians to nickname the engine Humpty Dumpty. This episode may have given rise to the two following lines in the English version of the rhyme, which is otherwise an age-old warning against lost virginity.

. . . All the King's horses, and all the King's men
Couldn't put Humpty together again.

The siege was raised on Thursday 7 September when the Earl of Essex, described by Corbet as the general, made his triumphal entry to the city:

His majesty was forced to leave the towne behinde him, and constrained to a tedious march in that tempestuous rainy night; their carriages were not got up the hills till the next morning, which distraction was not known to us: and the general's army was tired with long and continuall marches. The admirable care of Providence was beheld in the season of our reliefe, when all things were prepared by the enemy for a generall storme; our ammunition consumed, but three single barrels of powder left in our magazine, and not so much more elsewhere: in the little harm done by their cannon and mortar-pieces, that sent amongst us so many terrible messengers.

Our lost men taken or slain did not amount to the number of fifty; and of these but two officers were slain, Captain Harcus and the Governour's ensign; yet we killed of the enemy (who never ventured an assault) above a thousand men, by the lowest confession. The king expended much in ammunition, engines, and keeping together the discontented souldiers, besides the losse of his pretious time in that full tyde of victory. . .

On 5 September, as thousands of the Royalist army wearily marched up Painswick Hill, Charles is reputed to have been resting on a stone when one of his young sons asked him when they would be home. 'I have no home to go to,' replied the disconsolate king. Shortly afterwards his aides found him a safe house in which to rest the night, and though it was just a remote cottage the grateful monarch declared it Paradise. The hamlet where it stood remains Paradise to this day; for many years there was even an Adam and Eve pub to add piquancy to the name.

The Cotswolds' other major Civil War engagement was outside Stow-on-the-Wold on 21 March, 1646. Midway through the month Lord Astley received an order from the king to move troops from garrisons in Wales to Worcester. From there he was to take two thousand horses and foot to Oxford, to be met by fifteen hundred horse and foot on the road.

Letters and orders were intercepted, and the Roundheads grouped to force a battle – Colonel Birch with six hundred horse and foot from Hereford, Colonel Morgan's force from Gloucester and more men from Evesham; they lay in wait for the Royalists for six days at Stow, and on March 20 their patience was rewarded as they saw the foe climbing Broadway Hill.

They followed them through the night, reinforced by Sir William Brereton with a thousand horses from Lichfield, and

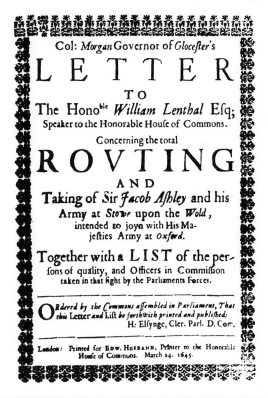

Col: *Morgan* Governor of *Glocefter's*

LETTER

TO

The Hono^ble *William Lenthal* Efq;
Speaker to the Honorable Houfe of Commons.

Concerning the total

ROVTING

AND

Taking of Sir *Jacob Afhley* and his Army at *Stow* upon the *Wold*, intended to joyn with His Majefties Army at *Oxford*.

Together with a LIST of the perfons of quality, and Officers in Commiffion taken in that fight by the Parliaments Forces.

Rdered by the Commons affembled in Parliament, That this Letter and Lift be forthwith printed and publifhed:
H: Elfynge, Cler. Parl. D. Com.

London: Printed for EDW. HUSBAND, Printer to the Honorable Houfe of Commons. March 24. 1645.

Stow-on-the-Wold

Burford

both armies drew up in battle form to await the light of day. The outnumbered Royalists fought valiantly, but lost the day with more than two hundred killed, and when the tattered remnants of their army retreated into Stow they had to contend with further skirmishes.

This letter, written on the day of the battle, was from Sir William Brereton to William Lenthall, Speaker of the House of Commons:

Sir,

God (blessed be His name) hath preserved us as gloriously and graciously this Day as in many of our former Great Mercies. After Two Nights and a Day's March I came up to Colonel Morgan and Colonel Birch about Three of the Clock this Morning (neare Stowe on Cotswole Hills). We fell on between Four and Five.

It was carried on somewhat doubtfully, and almost dangerously at first; but God renewed our Courage, gave us the Day, Sir Jacob Ashley Prisoner, some Colonels, Lieutenant Colonels also, and all the Foot with their Arms. Leisure will give the Particulars. God, that hath done all, must have all the Glory. The Lord increase our Thankfulness more and more.

Sir, I am
Your humble servant
William Brereton

Stowe, March 21st
7 a clock Morning

The Bearer, an Eye-witness, can say more; and myself testify the most gallant and valiant Behaviour of our Two above-named Colonels, Colonel Morgan and Birch.

The immediacy of Brereton's writing, at 7 o'clock on the morning of the dawn battle, seems to bring history alive. As Brereton was dashing off this note, men were still crying in agony

and dying. More than two hundred men had lost their lives in the previous two hours.

An aftermath of the Civil War in the Cotswolds was the Levellers incident at Burford in May 1649. Levellers were radical Roundhead soldiers who felt Cromwell was betraying the cause for which they had fought almost before the executed Charles I was cold in his grave, and after a group of them had mutinied in Salisbury they marched towards Banbury to meet up with other disaffected troops.

Cromwell and Fairfax caught them at Burford, and after a skirmish near the Crown at the corner of Sheep Street in which one man died, 340 Levellers were captured and imprisoned in the church on May 15. The signature of one of them, Antony Sedley, can still be seen scratched on the font.

All were told they would be executed. Instead, they were left to ponder their fate for three days, after which three of them paid the penalty while the others watched from the church roof. Cornet Thompson was the first to die. Then came Corporal Perkins who, according to a contemporary account, 'accounting it a great mercy that he was to die for this quarrel . . . so died gallantly as he had lived religiously'. The last to be shot, John Church:

Stretched out his arms, and bade the soldiers do their duty, looking them in the face, till they gave fire upon him, without the least kind of fear or terror.

A ringleader of the mutiny, Cornet Denne, was led out with them, but Cromwell reprieved him at the last moment. Instead, the relieved but doubtless still terrified soldier was forced to preach Cromwell's virtues to his fellows, an about-turn which the writer of a Leveller pamphlet of the time found beneath contempt:

They enjoin Denne to preach apostasy to us in the pulpit of Burford Church . . . and justify all those wicked and abominable proceedings of the General . . . howling and weeping like a crocodile, and to make him a perfect rogue and villain upon everlasting record.

A few miles further east along the Windrush Valley from Burford is the village of Minster Lovell, and it was here that Robert Plot discovered the strange and singular case of Rebeckah Smith, as documented in his work THE NATURAL HISTORY OF OXFORDSHIRE.

. . . [A strange] accident befel one Rebeckah Smith, the Servant-maid of one Thomas White of Minster Lovel, who being of a robust constitution, though she seldom eat flesh (it scarce agreeing with her) and above 50 years of age; after she came from the Communion on Palm Sunday, April 16. Anno 1671 was taken with such a dryness in her throat, that she could not swallow her spittle, nor anything else to supply the decays of nature: and in this case she continued without eating or drinking, to the amazement of all, for about ten weeks, viz. to the 29 of June, being both St. Peters, and Witney-fair day: by which time being brought very low, her master enquired and found out a person who gave him an Amulet (for it was supposed she was bewitch'd) against this evil; after the application whereof, within two or three days time (thought I dare not suppose there was any dependence between the medicine and disease) she first drank a little water, then warm broaths in small quantities at a time, and nothing else till Palm Sunday again twelve months after, when she began to eat bread and other food again as formerly she had done, and is now about the age of sixty, and still living at the same place ready to testifie the truth of the thing, as well as Tho. White and his wife, who were all that lived in the house with her, and will confidently assert (for they carefully observed) that they do not believe she ever took anything in those ten weeks time, nor any thing more all the year following but what was above-mentioned: wherein I think they may the rather be credited, because there was never any advantage made of this wonder, which argues it clear of all juggle or design.

In the same village lie the ruins of Minster Lovell Hall, the home in the fifteenth century of one of Richard III's closest friends, Francis, Viscount Lovell. On 18 July 1484 a seditious rhyme was fastened to the door of St Paul's Cathedral in London:

The Cat, the Rat, and Lovell our dog
Rule all England under an Hog.

The Cat was William Catesby, Richard's Chancellor of the Exchequer; the Rat was Sir Richard Ratcliffe, an influential member of Richard's inner council. Lovell our dog was Francis Lovell, whose family emblem was a hound. The Hog, of course, was Richard himself, his emblem being the white boar.

Francis Lovell was a boyhood friend of Richard, and one of his closest and most trusted supporters. Lovell escaped at the battle of Bosworth in 1485, when Richard lost his life, and in 1487 he joined forces with Richard's nephew John, Earl of Lincoln. They were defeated by Henry VII at the battle of Stoke in June of that year, and the last official news of Francis was that he was seen escaping from the field by swimming across the river Trent.

A letter from William Cowper to Francis Peck throws some light on his fate:

Hertingfordbury Park
9th August, 1737

Sir,

I met t'other day with a memorandum I had made some years ago, perhaps not unworthy of notice. You may remember that Lord Bacon, in his history of Henry VII, giving an account of the battle of Stoke, says of the Lord Lovell, who was among the rebels, that he fled and swame over the Trent on horseback, but could not recover the further side, by reason of the steepnesse of the bank, and so was drowned in the river. But another report leaves him not there, but that he lived long after, in a cave or vault.

Minster Lovell

Sheepscombe

Apropos to this; on the 6th May, 1728, the present Duke of Rutland related in my hearing that about twenty years then before, viz. in 1708, upon occasion of new laying a chimney at Minster Luvel, then was discovered a large vault underground in which was the entire skeleton of a man, as having been sitting at a table which was before him with a book, paper, pen, &c.; in another part of the room lay a cap, all much mouldered and decayed. Which the family and others judged to be this Lord Lovel, whose exit has hitherto been so uncertain.

C. Henry Warren takes up the story in his book A
COTSWOLD YEAR:

One day a workman was picking at one of the walls when he came upon a sealed doorway leading into a secret chamber near the chimney. The wall was opened, and there, in the little room inside, was a skeleton sitting at a table, with the Bible open before it. It was young Lord Lovell. Evidently there was only one way into the room, and when his attendant died, or was killed, he was left to starve in his secret hiding-place. Some say it was a woman who fed him for many years. . .

From Viscount Lovell we move on to the eighteenth century with one of England's most prolific writers, Daniel Defoe. His TOUR THROUGH THE WHOLE ISLAND OF GREAT BRITAIN *was published in parts from 1724 to 1726, when he was in his middle sixties:*

Wotton-under-Edge and Dursley

On the Right [*of the road from Bristol to Gloucester*] lies *Wotton*, a pretty Market-town, governed by a Mayor elected annually at the Court-Leet. 'Tis famous for its Cloathing trade. The Church, which is a Vicarage, is large, and hath Two wide Isles, and an high handsome Tower, adorned with Battlements and Pinacles. There are in it divers Tombs, Monuments, and Inscriptions, chiefly for the Family of *Berkley*. Here are a Freeschool, and some Charity-houses.

Directly North of this Town lies *Dursley*, a good Clothing and Market-town, governed by a Bailiff, and Four Constables; and has been formerly noted for sharp, over-reaching People; from whence arose a proverbial Saying of a tricking Man, *He is a Man of Dursley*. The Church is good, hath Two Isles, and an handsome Spire.

Cheltenham

From *Gloucester* we kept Eastward, and soon came to *Cheltenham*, a Market-town, where is still a pretty good Trade carried on in Malt, but not so considerable as formerly. Here is a good Church in the Form of a Cross, with Isles on each Side, and a Spire rising in the Middle, noted for a good Ring of-Bells. But what is more remarkable is, that the Minister is to be nominated by, and must be a Fellow of *Jesus-College*, Oxon (tho' the Vicarage is but 40*l.* a Year), but approved of by the Earl of *Gainsborough*; and he cannot hold it more than Six Years. Here are a Freeschool, an Hospital, and some other Charities.

The Mineral Waters lately discovered at *Cheltenham*, which are of the *Scarborough* Kind, are what will make this Place still more and more remarkable, and frequented. An eminent Physician has obliged me with the following Account of their Nature and Qualities:

These Waters, he observes, were first found out by the Flocks of all the neighbouring Pigeons going constantly thither to provoke their Appetites, as well as to quench the uncommon Thirst of these salacious Birds. I have been informed, says he, by a Physician of Credit and Experience, who had made all the common Trials on them, and observed their Effects on many Persons of various Consti-

tutions, and in different Distempers, who had drank them, That, on Evaporation, they were found to contain, in a Gallon, Eight Drachms of nitrous Salt, with Two Drachms of an alcalious Earth: That they were compounded of a large Quantity of Nitre, to which they owed their purgative Virtue; a light Sulphur, which the fetid Dejections manifested; and a volatile Steel, discoverable by a transparent blue Colour, when mixed with an Infusion of Nut-galls.

Alcalious Spirits have no Effect on them; but they ferment with Acids. He further adds That there might be found some other Materials in their Composition, perhaps, if more minutely examined and tortured: but that these mentioned Principles were evident and incontestable, and were sufficient to account for all their Effects and Operation; the others (if there be any) being of little Efficacy.

In the Operation, they empty the Bowels according to their Dose, but gently, mildly, and easily, without Sickness, Nausea, Gripes, or causing great Lowness, far beyond any artificial Purges whatsoever. They give a good Appetite, an easy Digestion, and quiet Nights, in all nephritic and gouty Cases, and when not under the Fit; in all rheumatic, scrophulous, scorbutic, or leprous Cases; but especially in spermatic, urinary, or haemorrheidal Cases, he thinks them sovereign, and not to be matched.

In a word, in all inflammatory Cases of whatever Kind, and whatever Part, he thinks them one of the most salutary Means which can be used. Those of pretty strong Nerves, and firm Constitutions, bear them with high Spirits, great Pleasure and Profit; but they do not all suit with those of weak Nerves, paralytic, hypochondriac, or hysteric Disorders, or those who are subject to any kind of Fits, Cramps, or Convulsions: they ruffle such too much, as generally all Purgatives do. He thinks they have a great Affinity to the *Scarborough* Waters, and might do great Cures in most chronical Distempers if Excercise and a proper Regimen were directed with them.

Frampton Mansell

A call from the miller

Stroud

Gloucestershire must not be passed over without some Account of a pleasant and fruitful Vale, which crosses Part of the County, from East to West, on that Side of the *Cotswolds*, and which is called *Stroud-water*; famous not only for the finest Cloths, but for dyeing those Cloths of the beautiful Scarlets, and other grand Colours, that are any-where in *England*, perhaps in any Part of the World. Here I saw Two Pieces of Broadcloth made, one Scarlet, the other Crimson in Grain, which were sent as Presents, the one to the late King *George*, while Elector, and the other to his present Majesty, which were very graciously accepted. The Cloth was valued at 45*s. per* Yard, and was well worth it; for nothing so rich of that Kind had ever been made in *England*, as I was informed.

Some thirty years after Defoe another visitor to pass through the Cotswolds was not so complimentary, especially about his overnight stay at the White Hart in Dursley. John Jackson, a Yorkshireman from Woodkirk in the West Riding, kept a diary of a journey he made to Glastonbury Thorn. This extract is from his journey home:

4 January 1756

At morn I left Philip Jones [*at Berkeley*] and went and took leave of my very good friend Mr. William Jenkins, and both found and left him sewing Sail Cloth, and I tarry'd a good while and we discoursed very freely, and I was very civilly entertained and had some copper coin given at my coming away. And so I set off for Dursley, and lodged at Robert Goodwins, the Sign of the White Hart in Dursley, and in Dursley is a neat beautiful Market House, and in this town I saw 2 swine lay killed and burnt as black as a toad, and one lay on a table and the other ith' mucky miry way, the ugliest object I thought that ever my eyes beheld, and that more of their cookery is more proper for dogs and swine than men. Their toad-back bacon and Cabbage-kettle stinking porrage like Traynoyl or like the stink of the Hog sty.

> God sends good meat, the Deel sends Cooks
> To spile and marr the same;
> With sulky, saucy, simpering looks,
> Maid, Mrs., and Mad Dame.

Toad-back-bacon is a Gloucestershire term for bacon that has been smoked in the chimney until it is black on the outside and hard within. Reference to the cabbage-kettle reflects a time when that vegetable was part of the staple diet. A pot of it would have been on the hob most of the time, gently simmering, with new leaves put in to replace what had been eaten. Presumably these kettles were not cleaned out as often as they might have been!

Another local delicacy was ag pag dump, supposedly a type of suet pudding flavoured with sloes. One Cotswold rhyme celebrates the dish as a speciality of the village of Nympsfield:

> Nympsfield is a pretty place
> Set upon a tump
> But all the people do live upon
> Is ag pag dump.

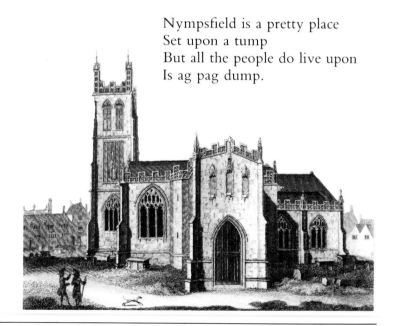

That great man of letters Horace Walpole hardly touched upon the Cotswolds, but he brushed past the hills in 1774 – and as is plain from this letter to the Rev. William Cole, he was not impressed:

Matson, near Gloucester Aug. 15, 1774

Dear Sir,

. . . Today I have been at Berkeley and Thornbury Castles. The first disappointed me much, though very entire. It is much smaller than I expected, but very entire, except a small part burnt two years ago, whilst the present Earl was in the house. The fire began in the housekeeper's room, who never appeared more; but as she was strict over the servants, and not a bone of her was found, it was supposed that she was murdered, and the body conveyed away.

The situation is not elevated nor beautiful, and little improvements made of late, but some silly ones *à la Chinoise*, by the present Dowager. In good sooth, I can give you but a very imperfect account; for, instead of the lord's being gone to dine with the mayor of Gloucester, as I expected, I found him in the midst of all his captains of the Militia.

I am so sillily shy of strangers and youngsters, that I hurried through the chambers, and looked for nothing but the way out of every room. I just observed that there were many bad portraits of the family, but none ancient; as if the Berkeleys had been commissaries, and raised themselves in the last war. There is a plentiful addition of those of Lord Berkeley of Stratton, but no knights templars, or barons as old as Edward I; yet are there three beds on which there may have been frisky doings three centuries ago, as there probably have been within these ten years.

The room shown for the murder of Edward II and the shrieks of an agonising king, I verily believe to be genuine. It is a dismal chamber almost at top of the house, quite detached, and to be approached only by a kind of foot-bridge, and from that descends a large flight of steps that terminate on strong gates; exactly a situation for a *corps de garde*. In that room they show you a cast of a face in plaster, and tell you it was taken from Edward's. I was not quite so easy of faith about that; for it is evidently the face of Charles I.

The steeple of the church, lately rebuilt handsomely, stands some paces from the body; in the latter are three tombs of the old Berkeleys, with cumbent figures. The wife of the Lord Berkeley, who was supposed to be privy to the murder, has a curious head-gear; it is like a long horse-shoe quilted in quatrefoils and, like Lord Foppington's wig, allows no more than the breadth of a half-crown to be discovered of the face. Stay, I think I mistake; the husband was a conspirator against Richard II, not Edward. But in those days loyalty was not so rife as present.

From Berkeley Castle I went to Thornbury, of which the ruins are half ruined. It would have been glorious, if finished. I wish the Lords of Berkeley had retained the spirit of deposing till Henry VIIIth's time! The situation is fine, though that was not the fashion, for all the windows of the great apartment look into the inner court. The prospect was left to the servants. Here I had two adventures. I could find nobody to show me about. I saw a paltry house that I took for the sexton's at the corner of the close, and bade my servant ring, and ask who could show me the castle.

A voice in a passion flew from a casement, and issued from a divine. 'What! Was it his business to show the Castle? Go look for somebody else! What did the fellow ring for as if the house was on fire?' The poor Swiss came back in a fright, and said the doctor had sworn at him. Well – we scrambled over a stone stile, saw a room or two

Dursley

Dursley

glazed near the gate, and rung at it. A damsel came forth and satisfied our curiosity.

When we had done seeing I said, 'Child, we don't know our way, and want to be directed into the London road; I see the Duke's steward yonder at the window, pray desire him to come to me, that I may consult him.' She went – he stood staring at us at the window, and sent his footman. I do not think courtesy is resident at Thornbury. As I returned through the close, the divine came running out of breath, and without his beaver or band, and calls out, 'Sir, I am come to justify myself: your servant says I swore at him: I am no swearer – Lord bless me! (dropping his voice) it is Mr. Walpole!'

'Yes, Sir, and I think you was Lord Beauchamp's tutor at Oxford, but I have forgot your name.'

'Holwell, Sir.'

'Oh! Yes.' And then I comforted him, and laid the ill-breeding on my footman's being a foreigner; but could not help saying I really had taken his house for the sexton's. 'Yes, Sir, it is not very good without, won't you please to walk in?' I did, and found the inside ten times worse, and a lean wife, suckling a child. He was making an Index to Homer, is going to publish the chief beauties, and I believe had just been reading some of the delicate civilities that pass between Agamemnon and Achilles, and that what my servant took for oaths, were only Greek compliments.

Adieu! Yours ever.

You see I have not a line more of paper.

The Rev. William Holwell, vicar of Thornbury, completed his book. It was published in 1776, under the brief title, of *EXTRACTS FROM MR. POPE'S TRANSLATION, CORRESPONDING WITH THE BEAUTIES OF HOMER, SELECTED FROM THE ILIAD.*

A far better known contemporary of the unworldly vicar was Gloucestershire's greatest historian, Samuel Rudder. A NEW HISTORY OF GLOUCESTERSHIRE was published in 1779, a mammoth work that lists parishes in alphabetical order. First comes a topographical description, followed by details of the ownership of the larger houses, the history of the manor and notes on the church and its monuments. These are a few descriptions:

Bibury

This is a parish of considerable extent in the Cotswold part of the county, six miles south from Northleach, seven north-eastward from Cirencester, and nineteen eastward from Gloucester. The tithing of Winson is in the hundred of Bradley, but all the rest of the parish lies in the hundred of Britwelsbarrow.

The name of this place, anciently written *Bechberie*, and *Begeberie*, seems to have been given it on account of the situation of the village upon the river; for bece or beke signifies a stream or river, and berie a flat piece of ground. The latter part of the name, if referred to the place where the church stands, agrees well enough with the situation; but some of the houses stand on the side of an eminence. Here the river Coln rises in so copious a manner as to drive a mill at a small distance from the head of a spring.

The turnpike-road from Cirencester to Oxford leads through this place, and where it crossed the river, the water was broad and deep, and being near the spring, so remarkably cold, as frequently to injure cattle, which, heated with travelling, passed through it; wherefore a bridge was erected by subscription a few years ago, to obviate those inconveniences.

Bisley

. . . There are two small brooks which run through the parish into Stroud river. The greater part of the parish is high ground, consisting mostly of arable and woodland, with extensive wastes, on which are several populous villages, inhabited chiefly by poor people employ'd in the clothing manufacture. But it is probable that is was not formerly much more woody than at present, and that its name is compounded of *bois*, a wood, and leaze, a pasture. Leaving this etymology to stand or fall as reason and better judgments may determine, I proceed to give a short description of such places as in this parish as more particularly deserve notice.

In the woodland part, on the northern border, lies a small sequestered glyn or valley, called *Timbercomb-bottom*, noted for its singular situation, being intirely separated from the rest of the world by thick surrounding woods, which make it not easily accessible, nor is it to be seen 'til you enter into it. It is an estate belonging to Mr Smart.

Chalford-bottom is a deepended narrow valley, about a mile in length, lying partly in Minchinhampton, but the greater part, being on the north side of the river which runs to Stroud, is in this parish. On the curious traveller's first approach, it presents at once a very striking and respectable appearance, consisting of a great number of well-built houses, equal to a little town, lying very contiguous, but not joined together. These are intermixt with rows of tenters, along the side of the hill, on which the cloth is stretched in the process of making. This variety of landscape is uncommonly pleasing, and so great and surprising is the acclivity where some of the buildings stand, that in different approaches to the same house, you ascend to the lowest story, and descend to the highest. In this bottom are eight fulling-mills, and here, and the villages above the hill, called the *Linches*, within the parish, great numbers of people, employed in the different branches of woollen manufacture, reside. But the trade has lately been very much on the decline. . . .

Arlington Mill, Bibury

Swan Hotel, Bibury

Bourton-on-the-Water

. . . This village is situate about a quarter of a mile south-east from the Roman foss, in a fertile vale, surrounded by hills at a pleasing distance, and is watered by a river, which rises a little above it, and, as it enters the village, forms itself into an elegant serpentine canal about thirty feet wide, flowing with an agreeable rapidity, about the depth of fourteen or fifteen inches.

Many of the houses are ranged into a street, tho' somewhat irregularly, on each side of this natural canal, the banks of which being well gravelled, and very rarely over-flow'd, afford a delightful walk. The river is remarkable for fine trout, eel, and crayfish. In the centre of the place is a handsome freestone bridge of three arches, built in 1756, beside which there are several wood bridges for foot passengers, at such distances as to render the communication perfectly commodious. There is a good raised road carried through the place; but it is to be regretted, that some of the best houses are not arranged in the street, which would have made a great addition to the agreeable appearance of this handsome village.

Nature has been lavish with her favours to this place, and with a little more of the assistance of her younger sister, Art, it might vie in beauty and elegance with any Dutch village. Many topographers have made no mention of it, and none have done it justice; for tho' it has not a market, here are shops for the supply of goods, and the more necessary kinds of trade are carried on as in a market town; and there is reason to believe, that it has been much larger and more populous than at present, for there are many foundations still visible, which are undoubtedly the ruins of houses, as may be concluded from the ashes of wood and coal that are found about them. . . .

Cirencester

. . . On a near approach to the town, there is a gentle descent every way, except from the south. The air is so remarkably pure and salubrious that a physician who settled here about forty years since, after staying a time sufficient, as he thought, to make trial of his success, pronounced it impossible for one of his profession to subsist on the practice the town and its neighbourhood afforded. The water is sufficiently pure and pleasant, rising in a fine gravel, about fourteen or fifteen feet below the surface, and almost every house has a pump.

. . . Coming into the town from Gloucester, a great part of the street is a hollow way, in some places five feet deep, where a portion of the Churn water runs, and empties itself into one of the arms of that river at the second bridge. There is a tradition that the river anciently ran through the middle of the town . . . And not many years since, as the workmen were digging a vault under the street, near where the four principal streets meet, at about the depth of six feet under the surface, they found stones set up edge-ways, like those commonly placed in a water-course, for people to step on. This circumstance, I

think, puts the matter out of doubt, that anciently the water ran through the town by the high cross, and so down Cricklade-street, and at length joined the main river at Watermore.

There is a great deal of travelling through this place from the northern to the western parts of England, and from Bath and Bristol to London, through Oxford and Abingdon. Two stage-coaches pass thro' it to London, and a third in its course between Bath and Oxford; which, with a great number of heavy carriages that keep their regular stages, open a communication between this place and Monmouthshire, South Wales, Hereford, Gloucester, Worcester, Warwick, Coventry, Leicester, Nottingham, the West, and many other places; a circumstance so favourable to trade, that, next to Gloucester, this is esteemed the principal market-town in the county.

A farmyard at Coln St. Dennis

Bourton-on-the-Water

Coln St. Aldwyn

. . . The river *Coln*, increased by the Bibury water, runs reluctantly through this parish, with a slow stream; and the trout grows in it to a good size, whereas at Bibury 'tis always light and slender. . . . This is a pretty little village. The lands rise in a bold manner on each side of the Coln, and the church and houses are seen pleasantly situated on the north-east side, overlooking the river, the stone bridge upon which is part repaired by this parish, and part by Quenington. . . .

Hasleton

. . . It is situated high on the Coteswolds, with a fine healthy air. The country hereabout is almost destitute of trees, and so much exposed to the winds from every quarter, that vegetation is not a little retarded. The soil is generally light and stony, and mostly in tillage; yet agriculture is lately so much improved in this open, I had almost said naked region, that the farmers obtain good crops of corn, and feed and fat great numbers of sheep, and some black cattle; and many of them keep a little dairy besides. The parish hath lately been inclosed, and it is hoped that, as well for profit as ornament, planting of beech, ash, and fir, which suit the soil, may take place with other improvements. . . .

Hawling

. . . This village, which lies in an open champain country, is said to be one of the highest places on the Coteswolds, and is remarkable for its healthy air, sound sheep, and sweet mutton. Husbandry is the chief employment of the male inhabitants, but the women and children spin woollen yarn for the clothiers. The common fields in this parish, containing 977 acres, were inclosed by act of parliament in the year 1756.

Stow-on-the-Wold

. . . It is a market town, situated, in a very peculiar manner, on the summit of a high hill, about three miles diameter in base, and exposed to every inclemency of the weather, without the least shelter or protection. The base of the hill is encircled by a kind of narrow valley, and the great Roman Foss Way runs a little northward of the town.

It is commonly said, that *Stow wants three elements out of the four*. It wants water, from its high situation, and having little or no land belonging to the town, and consequently no produce of fewel, it is deficient in earth and fire; but it has air enough, which in this mountainous and exposed situation, must necessarily be very sharp and piercing, tho' pure, and perhaps, for strong constitutions, healthy. The church is pretty lofty, and as there is nothing to obstruct the view, it is seen like a land mark, from every place for many miles all round that part of the country.

The town is small, and very irregularly built, with two or three mean houses in the midst of the principal street. It has a weekly market on Thursday, pretty well frequented; and two fairs in the year, held, since the rectification of our Calendar, on the 12th of May, and the 24th of October, for all sorts of cattle, hops, cheese, Birmingham wares, linen of the manufacture of this part of the country, and other valuable commodities. The fairs were formerly very large, but are much declined; tho' it is said, that the tolls of them, and of the markets, are at present worth £80 a year. . . .

Stroud

. . . The parish is in some places five miles long, and two broad, and consists of high grounds, and declivities thence on all sides to the waters, where the meadow and pasture lands are. Above them, the soil being mostly light and stony, is employ'd in tillage; but the upper part of the declivities consists of beech woods, which are continually suffering a diminution by the incroachment of the husbandman, and a desire of turning the land to a more immediate account.

The intermixture of gently rising hills and dales, with woods and lawns, produces in this country a great variety of pleasing landscapes and prospects, still heightened and improved by the beautiful tints of fine woollen cloths stretched upon the tenters, and villages of good stone buildings, all whitened, every where interspersed, and almost contiguous; so that strangers are greatly struck with the prospects, and think them superior to most they have seen.

Within the parish there is a market-town of the same name, situated on the ridge of a declivity, near the confluence of the river Froom and the Slade-water, in the midst of the principal clothing country of Gloucestershire, with which it maintains a good trade; but there is not much travelling through it, because of the steep hills that encompass it almost on every side except to the westward. It is not large, in proportion to the populousness of the country; for the clothiers don't reside in the town, but generally near the rivulets where their respective mills stand; whence the *Bottoms*, as they are called, are an almost continued range of houses and villages, and from the hills exhibit a most pleasing view of a populous country. . . .

. . . The trade of this part of the country, tho' frequently fluctuating, is in general considerable. They make here a great variety of broad clothes, both for home consumption and foreign trade, from those of low value to the best Spanish. These are sent away either white, or dyed in the cloth; and in particular great quantities are dyed scarlet, for which branch of trade the place is noted. The beauty of their colours is very great, to the perfection of which the Froom water has been erroneously supposed to contribute, for it is most assuredly owing to the skill of the artist.

Many hands are employ'd in the various branches of the manufacture, as in cleansing the wool by picking and washing it; in scribbling and spinning it; spooling and warping the yarn; weaving the cloth; burling, milling, and rowing it; then in shearing and dressing it; and, if to be sent off coloured, in dying it; and lastly, in pressing and packing it; and most of these processes are carried on by distinct workmen.

As spinning requires most hands, some of the clothiers send their wool to the distance of twenty miles or more, and the poor women and children, for that extent of country, work at this branch, which makes it difficult to ascertain the numbers employ'd in the manufacture. Most of the other branches are carried on at the mills, or at the clothiers houses; but the weavers work at home. There are in this parish eighteen clothing mills, and about thirty master clothiers.

The editor of the *Magna Britannia* estimates the returns of the clothiers of these parts at £50,000 *per ann.* 'some making,' says he, '1000 clothes a year for their own share.' What he means by *these parts* is not very certain, but his calculation is much too low, and especially for the present time; for the cloth made annually within this parish only is supposed to amount to near £200,000, and there is one person that makes above 3000 clothes a year. Very large fortunes have been acquired in this business, and it is an observation of Mr. Camden's that several of the most eminent families among the nobility in this nation have had their rise from it. . . .

Whittington

This parish lies in the hundred of Bradley, near five miles south-eastward from Cheltenham, five south from Winchcombe, thirteen north from Cirencester, and thirteen east from Gloucester.

It is a small parish, in the Coteswold country, consisting

The River Coln at Fairford

Eastleach

of more arable than pasture ground. The village is shel-
tered on the north by some very lofty fields, whose tops
are adorned with plantations of firs. The Coln, a very
pretty trout river, rises in a small head at this place, and
growing more considerable, gives name to several villages
thro' which it passes in its course to Fairford, where it
empties itself into the Thames. . .

Willersey

This is a small parish, in the upper division of Kiftsgate hundred, about three miles west from Chipping Campden, five south-eastward from Evesham, and twenty-six north-eastward from Gloucester.

The village is seated in the Vale, and lies under the west side of those hills which every where mark the limits of the Coteswold country with a bold and well defined outline. On the summit of the hill above the village, but within the parish, there is a large camp, inclosing about sixty acres of ground, supposed to have been formed in the time of the Danish ravages, and it still continues pretty perfect.

From this camp there is a fine bird's-eye view of the vale below, intersected with beautiful hedge-rows, and scattered with villages and farm houses. The river Avon meanders through the middle of the vale, and the town of Evesham at an agreeable distance, presents itself as the principal object, with the Breedon and Malvern hills in the back ground to close the view. This camp and prospect principally distinguish Willersey; but in prosecuting my inquiry after curiosities, I was informed by the rector, as a matter worthy notice, that there is an estate here, subject to a rent-charge proportioned by the rate of the land-tax, payable to a certain family as a recompense (tho' an inadequate one) for preserving the life of king Charles the Second, by hiding him in the oak. When the land-tax is at three shillings in the pound, the annuity, or payment, is four guineas.

Windrush

Lies in the hundred of Slaughter, about nine miles distant southward from Stow-on-the-Wold; four westward from Burford in Oxfordshire, and twenty-four east from Gloucester.

It enjoys a healthy air, and consists chiefly of corn fields. The lands decline on the north side to the banks of a pretty river of the same name, which bounds the parish, and produces trout and cray fish; and after visiting Burford and Witney in Oxfordshire, empties itself into the Thames at a place called the New-bridge. . . .

Wotton-under-Edge

The town of Wotton-under-Edge is situated upon a pleasant eminence, overlooking a comb, or little valley, to the north-eastward. It lies near the foot of a ridge of hills to the north, which being partly covered with woods, have a very pleasing appearance. Hence the town certainly obtained its name, which is easily resolved into *Wood-town-under-ridge*. It is quite open to the other quarters, with an ample vale richly beset with villages and farm houses before it, and commanding an extensive and beautiful prospect, including the populous parish of Kingswood, formerly famous for its monastery, the towns of Wickwar and Sodbury, with Lansdown hill near Bath on one hand, and Berkeley castle, the Severn, Dean forest, and the Welch mountains on the other. . .

. . . It is pretty well built, and the clothing business, chiefly in the fine way, is of very ancient standing. There are now seven or eight master clothiers, and the trade is still in a flourishing state, tho' not equal to what it has sometimes been.

The market is held on Friday, and there is a fair on the 25th of September, formerly noted for cheese and cattle; but now of much less account for either.

The hills on one side of the town rendering it difficult for carriages to pass and repass, is a circumstance unfavourable to its market, which like that of most other little towns, is dwindled to nothing. There is, however, a turnpike-road branching from it northward to Gloucester, and eastward to Tetbury, and another extending south-westward towards Wickwar, Sodbury, and Bristol; but these are not the great roads leading from Gloucester to

Broadway

Stanton

Bath and Bristol; so that there is but little travelling through the town, except by people of the neighbourhood, and by such as are connected in trade with the inhabitants.

A point of interest in Rudder is the fact that, almost for the first time in our extracts, he comments on the natural beauty of the scenery around towns and villages. This was the time, with the Industrial Revolution gathering a head of steam, when sensitive observers were beginning to realise that trees and grass and flowers were no longer commodities merely to be taken for granted. It is true that Leland in the sixteenth century described many a village as pretty, but he was commenting strictly on its streetscape qualities, with communities showing signs of prosperity scoring most heavily with him.

Apart from his descriptions, Rudder sometimes passes an opinion on social conditions. Usually they are derogatory, as with his entries for the adjoining villages of Coaley and Uley, the latter being the parish of his birth.

Coaley

The public roads here are the worst that can be conceived; and the poor labouring people are so abandoned to nastiness, that they throw every thing within a yard or two of their doors, where the filth makes a putrid stench, to the injury of their own health, and the annoyance of travellers, if any come among them. The better houses are gone to ruin, and there is not a gentleman resident in the parish; but this is not peculiar to Coaley. . .

Uley

This village, tho' not large, is very populous, from a manufacture of fine broad cloth long established here. It is still carried on by several persons in a very extensive manner, and furnishes employment for the lower class of people. But idleness and debauchery are so deeply rooted in them, by means of those seminaries of vice called Alehouses, that the poor are very burthensome. These houses are scattered all over the country, and are daily increasing, which we owe either to the magistrates' inattention, or indulgence; or, perhaps, to a mistaken notion of serving the community by increasing the public revenue from licences; but they may be assured that nothing can compensate for depravity of morals, and the loss of industry.

Many customs had died out, or had been forced out by the Puritans, Dover's Games and the Stinchcombe Revels among them. Rudder notes some that managed to survive the repression, including those like the Randwick Mop which live on to this day.

Childswickham

. . . Here is a custom from time immemorial, for the lord of the manor to give a certain quantity of malt to brew ale to be given away at Whitsuntide and a certain quantity of flour to make cakes; every one who keeps a cow sends curds, others plums, sugar, and flour; and the payers to church and poor contribute 6*d.* each towards furnishing out an entertainment, to which every poor person of the parish who comes, has, with a quart of ale, a cake, a piece of cheese, and a cheesecake. . .

Randwick

. . . At this place an annual revel is kept on the Monday after Low Sunday, probably the wake of the church, attended with much irregularity and intemperance, and many ridiculous circumstances in the choice of a *Mayor*, who is yearly elected on that day, from amongst the meanest of the people. They plead the prescriptive right of ancient custom for the licence of the day, and the authority of the magistrate is not able to suppress it. . .

An unsigned letter in the GENTLEMAN'S MAGAZINE for May 1784 gives more information on the Randwick Mop . . .

As I was last year passing through the village of Randwic, near Stroud, in Gloucestershire, my attention was attracted by a crowd of people assembled round a horse pond, in which I observed a man, on whom I imagined the country people were doing justice in that summary way for which an English mob is so famous, though I was the same time surprised to hear them singing, as I thought, a psalm, since I never knew that to be part of the form of such judicial proceedings.

I soon, however, was informed of my error, and learned that it being 2d Monday after Easter, the people of the parish were assembled, according to an annual custom (the origin of which no one could tell me), to keep a revel. One of the parish is, it seems, on the above-mentioned day, elected mayor, and carried with great state, colours flying, drums beating, men, women, and children shouting, to a particular horse pond, in which his worship is placed, seated in an arm-chair; a song is then given out line by line by the clerk, and sung with great gravity by the surrounding crowd.

The Lord Mayor of Randwic's Song.

When Archelus began to spin,
And Pollo wrought upon a loom,
Our trade to flourish did begin,
Tho' Conscience went to selling broom.
When princes' sons kept sheep in field,
And queens made cakes with oaten flour,
And men to lucre did not yield,
Which brought good cheer to every bower.
But when the giants, huge and high,
Did fight with spears like weavers' beams,
And men in iron beds did lie,
Which brought the poor to hard extremes:

When cedar trees were grown so rife,
And pretty birds did sing on high;
Then weavers lived more void of strife
Than princes of great dignity.
Then David with a sling and stone,
Not fearing great Goliath's strength,
He pierc'd his brains, and broke his bones,
Though he was nine feet and a span in length.

Chorus
Let love and friendship still agree
To hold the bonds of amity.

The instant it is finished the mayor breaks the peace by throwing water in the face of his attendance. Upon this much confusion ensues; his worship's person is, however, considered sacred, and he is generally the only man who escapes being thoroughly souced. The rest of that day, and often of the week, is devoted to riot and drunkenness. The county magistrates have endeavoured, but in vain, to put a stop to this practice. The song was given me by the clerk of the parish, who said it had never been written before. It wants, you observe, some explanation.

Another famous Cotswold Whitsun Ale still celebrated today is the cheese-rolling at Cooper's Hill, about which more later. And it was close to Cooper's Hill in 1788 that King George III left his 'picture on a dish'. From an entry in the diary of Thomas Gardner, Sir John Dorington related the following anecdote:

George III, his Queen, and some of his children, visited Cranham or the neighbourhood in July 1788. A very aged woman, who did not know who her visitors were, came from her cottage to the carriage door and presented the old gentleman and his lady with a dish of bright red fragrant woodland strawberries. The old gentleman graciously accepted the welcome present. The dish was quickly cleared of its simple luxury.

Arlington Row, Bibury

Arlington Row, Bibury

The old woman stood by for her dish, and curtsied most respectfully and politely when it was returned. The old woman imagined it was the Squire and his family come to live at the great house. As the old woman held out her hand to receive the empty dish, the gentleman said in a most polite and affectionate manner, 'I am very much obliged to you for your great kindness.'

'You be mortal welcome,' replied the old woman, 'but I don't know who ye be – the Squire I spose?'

'No, my good woman, I have left my picture on the dish.'

The carriage drove back towards Cheltenham, and the woman returned to her cottage. When she put her empty dish upon her cottage table, she saw a 'golden guinea' glittering on the plate. 'I thought he said he had put his pic'tur on the dish. Well, I never know'd such a thing. This be a pretty pic'tur.' I cannot pretend to give her exact words. I may have copied them, and they may be preserved in my chaotic collection. I have given the shadow if not the substance of the dialogue. His picture or his portrait was on the coin. The old woman was subsequently astonished to find that she had seen 'The King, good old Varmer George.'

The expression, 'The King's picture' was frequently used in my boyhood. An aged gentleman said to me: twenty years ago, whenever I went to public dinners, friends often said, 'Weight, how is it that waiters pay you more attention than they do us?' 'It is plain enough. I al'us show 'um the King's pic'tur.'

The most interesting part of this letter is the reference to Cranham and the king's picture, for two later writers about Sapperton bear witness to the fact that a verbal tradition that he played the same trick there survived until well into this century.

The first was E. Temple Thurston in THE FLOWER OF GLOSTER, published in 1911 and a book to which we shall pay more attention later:

At the top of the valley, looking down between the hills through a lattice-work of apple blossom, stands the Bricklayers' Arms, a little inn with two or three houses clustered round it. An old man there described to me the opening of the tunnel in the reign of George IV. He had not seen it himself.

'My big grandfather' – this was how he told it to me – 'my big grandfather, the day the tunnel was opened, he was walking down the tow-path, and he met a feller coming along, and he said to my big grandfather, 'Where are you going, my man?'

'I'm going to see the king,' he says.

'I am the king,' says the man, and gives him a guinea; and when he looked on the head of the coin, I'm dommed if it worn't.'

Temple Thurston is wrong, of course, in crediting the story to George IV. The tunnel was opened to traffic in 1789 and formally blessed by George III three years later.

The story is told in more detail by the furniture maker Norman Jewson in his reminiscence BY CHANCE I DID ROVE, first published in 1951. He first came to the Cotswolds in 1907, and he was looking back to those early years – in other words, just the time that Temple Thurston was writing THE FLOWER OF GLOSTER – when he wrote:

Just before the bridge is a cottage belonging to the Canal Company, while on the far side is the Bricklayers' Arms, an inn built for the refreshment of the tunnel navvies. There used to be a large man-trap hanging on the wall near the entrance. Adjoining it is a cottage where at that time lived an old man named Cainey.

His proudest possession was a spade guinea, which he had inherited together with its history. The story, as he told it, was that his grandfather happened to be near the entrance to the tunnel one day, just after it was finished, when he saw several gentlemen on the towing path. One of the gentlemen called him up and asked him to guess who he was. Cainey replied that he didn't know, whereupon the gentleman pulled out a guinea from his pocket and told him to look at it, 'and he looked at him and he looked at the guinea, and sure as sure the gentleman's face and the face on the guinea were as like as two peas.'

These two reports build up an amusing picture of the old man at the tunnel entrance, eighty or so years ago, buttonholing all comers with this tale. He must have been disappointed when traffic fell away in later years, and the canal closed in 1911. Perhaps most interesting of all, though, is the way in which this little story, no doubt helped by the presence of the coin as a souvenir, lived as a verbal tradition from 1792 until at least the mid-1970s, when Norman Jewson died. Indeed there are probably folks alive today who remember old Cainey boring all and sundry with the tale in their childhood – a tale all but two hundred years old.

A year after 'Varmer George' visited the Cotswolds in 1788 another farmer, William Marshall, first published his RURAL ECONOMY OF GLOCESTERSHIRE. He had lived in Surrey and Norfolk and as he was well acquainted with such other counties as Yorkshire and Devon he had the advantage over Rudder of being able to add a comparative flavour to his writings.

Most of his work relates to the vales of Gloucester and Berkeley, but there is a sizeable section on the Cotswolds. In commenting on the vale and the western escarpment of the Cotswolds he is generally offended, like Rudder, by the ale houses, though he is pleased to note that they are not too numerous:

The only circumstance noticeable, in this place, is the unfrequency of alehouses, in the townships of the vale: a circumstance which reflects much honor on the magistracy of this county. Alehouses are an intolerable nuisance to husbandry. They are the nurseries of idleness, and every other vice. A virtuous nation could not, perhaps, be debauched sooner, or with more certainty, than by planting alehouses in it: yet we see them every where planted, as if for the purpose of rendering this nation more vicious than it already is.

If a reform of the lower class of people be really wished for, the first step towards it would be, to shut up the principal part of the petty alehouses which are, at present, authorized by Government to debauch them. Unfortunately, however, for so desirable a reform, alehouses, like lotteries, are opened 'for the good of the nation'! The nation must be in a tottering state, indeed, if it require gambling and drunkenness, the two main pillars of vice, to support it. . .

Most of Marshall's comments relate strictly to agriculture, but there are some general asides on the Cotswolds:

. . . It strikes me, forcibly, that the corners and asperities of every estate ought to be cut off, and the angles filled up with coppice wood; and that the more central farms ought each of them to have its skreen coppices; sufficiently extensive to admit of a plot being felled every year, for the use of the farm, and the cottagers of the township it lies in.

In winter, the poor, on these shelterless hills, must be in a wretched state, as to fuel. There are few hill countries which do not afford either wood, coals, peat, or at least turf; but, here, straw may be said to be the only fuel the country at present produces. Fortunately for the farmers, stone walls will not readily burn. . . .

. . . The climate of the Cotswold hills, when we consider their natural elevation, and their present nakedness, is unusually mild. I found vegetation, in May, nearly as forward, in the centre of this upland district, as in the richer warmer lands, in the neighbourhood of Glocester.

It is however remarked, by men of observation, that these hills vary much, as to their natural warmth. Spring

Workers in the hay field

Three-horse team, turning on the headland

snows are observed to pass off some of them much quicker than others. This is an evidence that climature depends on *soil*, or on something which is beneath the soil, rather than on what is generally termed the *air* . . .

In water, the Cotswold hills, considering their height, are singularly happy. Almost every dip has its rill, and every valley its brook. The sides of the hills abound with springs; and, even on the highest swells, water is generally found within the reach of a pump. Benefits, those, with which few upland countries are blessed. . . .

. . . Laborers are remarkably numerous, for the nature of the country; and their wages as remarkably low. A shilling a day (no beer) in autumn, winter, and spring. Fourteen pence, in hay time; except for mowing 18*d.*; and 2*s.* a day, for five weeks certain, in harvest. Women, in autumn and spring, 6*d.* in hay time 7*d.* in harvest 1*s.* No beer; except what is given voluntarily.

Servants' wages are likewise low: ten pounds the highest. Second men so low as five or six pounds. The standing food of farmers' servants, here, is bacon; with which they are allowed vegetables: a salutary accompaniment, which these most useful members of society are, perhaps through a mistaken policy, debarred from, in some districts. . . .

. . . The Cotswold laborers are expert, and indefatigable, in the work of 'breast-plowing' – the most slavish work of husbandry. The paring, burning, and spreading, have been done for 15*s.* an acre, from 15 to 20*s.* the common price, *notwithstanding the stoniness of the soil*. In some districts the paring alone would cost as much.

Paring for plowing under is sometimes got done in winter, a leisure season, so low as 5 to 7*s.* an acre. When sods, intended to be burnt, have been caught in a rainy season, as they are liable to be in every country, and have grown to the ground by lying a length of time upon it, they have been turned back again for half a crown an acre. An admirable operation, this, when it can be done at so low an expence. . .

During the Napoleonic Wars, the opportunities for well-off young men to take the Grand Tour to the Continent were greatly reduced, and often totally impossible. It was during this period that many of the upper classes took to discovering their own country, and keeping journals of their visits.

One was Sir Richard Colt Hoare of Stourhead, Wiltshire. After his wife's death in 1784 he spent six years travelling Europe until, in his own words, 'Continental war put a stop to these projects'. Between 1793 and 1810 he journeyed instead through Wales and England, touching on the Cotswolds:

Tuesday 21 June 1796

Left Orchardley, breakfasted at Bath, dined at Rodborough. Beautiful country, much peopled, great cloth manufacture. Walked to the churchyard where further great excavations are making to ascertain the limits of a Roman villa of which great vestiges have been found, and will be published, under the inspection of Mr. Lysons.

Arrived in the evening at Cheltenham. Delightful drive from Rodborough. Lodged at the Plough, a good inn.

Wednesday 22 June

Took a lodging at Mr Pope's, pleasantly situated not far from the well or town, yet quite in the country as to prospect and retirement. Terms: two guineas a week, viz half a guinea each for two rooms for myself, the same for one for my servant and the kitchen; the usual price of the lodgings here during the Summer season. The place begins to fill with company.

. . . The hills afford a constant variety of the most rich, extensive, beautiful views I ever beheld; not to be equalled in any part of England I have visited but in Devonshire on the hills beyond Exeter near Teignmouth . . .

Tetbury

Painswick

Rides:

To Tewkesbury eight miles. The abbey, lately new fitted up. Several curious monuments. The largest parish church in England except St. Albans. Venerable Saxon architecture.

To Gloucester nine miles. The cathedral. The new gaol, well worth visiting; its good arrangement, cleanliness and management; cost £26,000, raised by the county. Llanthony Abbey in ruins half a mile out of town and adjoining the new canal from Berkeley. Little of the building remains except a magnificent barn and part of the entrance gateway with three escutcheons with arms over it. One of them the arms of Bohun, Earl of Hereford. . . . Half a mile beyond Llanthony Abbey is Newark, a large house situated on an eminence, commanding a fine view of the city and environs, said to have belonged formerly to the Prior of the Abbey. . . .

Winchcomb, a long scattered village. Numbers of children in the streets. Remains of the abbey enclosure, well built. Grotesque heads about the church. No very curious monuments. An ancient house adjoining the churchyard now converted into a poorhouse. Inn: White Hart; tolerable.

Sudeley Castle, belonging to Lord Rivers. Fine ruin but not very picturesque; few points of view in which it appears to advantage. Chapel the most perfect part of the building. Some part of it appears as a castellated mansion, the other as a place of defence or fort. An uncommon fine crop of cone wheat in the left hand field leading from the town to the castle, some of it higher than my head, six feet at least. Remains of a noble barn.

Hales Abbey, two miles beyond Sudeley; bad road. Situated on a fine rich plain, surrounded by hills. The remains of the abbey trifling, yet worth visiting. It was formerly a rich mitred abbey. . . .

To Charlton Kings, seat and park of Mr Hunt. Old London Road, up the hill to the seven springs, supposed to be source of the River Thames; return by the Ballon public house and the Bath Road. . . .

I made an excursion to Park Corner, a tolerable inn. From thence to Sapperton a mile and half: famous tunnel of the canal through the hill. From thence through Oakley Woods to Cirencester 5 miles. Noble plantations, the work of one man, Lord Bathurst. Ten vistas meet at one broad point. The left-hand walk leads to Cirencester . . . a large town. Fine porch to the cathedral [*parish church*]; not many curious monuments, those of Brydges and Master the most so. Hungerford chapel more richly ornamented in its ceiling than the rest of the church. One pointed window. From Cirencester to Fairford 8 miles; beautiful church. Time of Henry vii . . . river made a fine sheet of water, full of trout. Good hothouses.

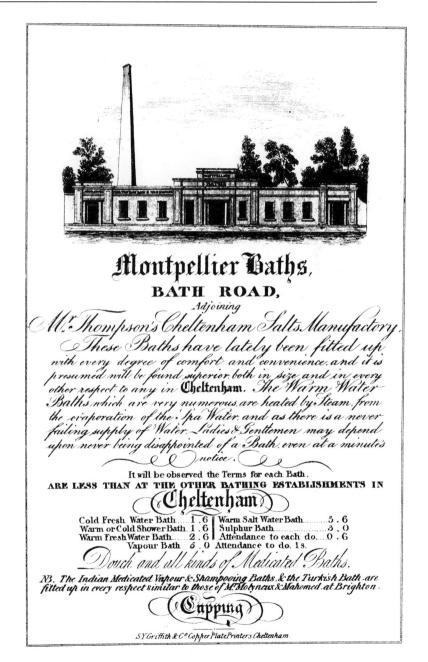

The Chipping Steps, Tetbury

The Thames & Severn Canal at Coates

To Painswick, eleven miles by Birdlip, one of the pleasantest rides in England, through a wild forest of beech wood and juniper bushes. A noble view from an old camp, double-ditched, a mile from Painswick. . . .

The carriage roads near Cheltenham are in general bad, except those leading through the vales to Gloucester and Tewkesbury. The country is very accessible on horseback and without a horse the finest views (perhaps in England) cannot be seen to advantage. The country well peopled and cultivated, the soil sandy and absorbent. The cone wheat, or bearded, is in general sown, a proof of the goodness of the land; it sells at a higher price and yields more per acre.

The vales are a very deep clay with a mixture of sand. Great tracts of beans, few oats and little barley. Those grains mostly cultivated in the Cotswold Hills, looking

over these rich vales. The hill farmers reckoned better than in the vales; land in the vales (arable) letts for thirty shillings and upwards (a tenant of Lord Sherborne's rents above 4,000 acres in this country). . .

From the hills (owing to the quantity of the trees in the hedgerows) the country bears a very woody appearance; few houses are distinguished. But on riding through the lanes in the plain the population and wealth of the yeo-manry and peasants show themselves, and, if I may judge from the appearance and frequent succession to each other, the farms are of moderate extent. The soil seems particularly adapted to the growth of trees; elms and oaks grow to a very great size. The fields and hedgerows are in general very well wooded. There are few large copses. Property much divided.

Chedworth

The Devil's Chimney, Leckhampton

Way of Life:

Spa opens at seven in the morning. Company meets from that time to nine.

Plays: Tuesday, Thursday, Saturday (Best actors and actreses: Rupell, Old Shute, and Mrs Bonneville and Mr Fox).

Balls: Monday and Friday. (Balls end at eleven at night).

Rooms for cards every night.

Rooms for tea on Sundays.

Bowling Green for ditto on ditto.

A coffee room with newspapers at the Plough Inn for gentlemen: subscription 5s. Sun, Star, Times and Morning Post.

(For drinking the waters usual price 5s. per week; a fee to Mrs Forster who pumps it; 5s. for the music; 2s. 6d. for the walks; and a guinea to the master of ceremonies).

No public ordinary as at Harrogate. The town well-paved; the lodgings in general very neat and clean; provisions plentiful and not extravagant in their price.

Colt Hoare's description of the Roman villa refers to Woodchester, where in excavations between 1793 and 1796 Samuel Lysons uncovered sixty-four rooms around three courtyards. In Gloucester, the new prison was completed in 1796 through the efforts of Sir George Onesiphorus Paul, a tireless prison reformer.

The comments about the new canal from Berkeley were rather optimistic; work was started in 1794, but after a long and troubled history it did not finally open until 1827, falling short of Berkeley by meeting the Severn at Sharpness. The Ballon was the Air Balloon between Birdlip and Crickley Hill, still a popular pub and landmark.

The only other notable Cotswold entries in his journal come in 1801, before a journey to North Wales. The following are edited from his journals from Thursday 16 April to Monday 11 May:

Thursday 16 April

. . . Passed Lord Suffolk's seat a little beyond Malmesbury. Cotswold sheep very like the Leicester breed. Thick coarse wool. A small compact sheep. Saw the double-furroe ploughs close to Cirencester in the middle of barley sowing.

Dined at Cirencester. Passed the Foss Road. Canal of the Stroud Navigation. Machines erected to try for coal. Fine church at Cirencester, beautiful southern porch of rich Gothic architecture. Ram Inn, old house, civil treatment. Many Roman antiquities have been found at this place which was a celebrated Roman station called *Corinium*. Many Roman roads led here. From hence to Birdlip . . . from Birdlip to Cheltenham.

Cirencester

The Thames & Severn Canal at the Golden Valley

Friday 17 April

Slight rain. Engaged in looking out for lodgings. Took those at Birch's at 2½ guineas per week and 18*s*. cook and house maid. Quiet, retired house though in the center of the town.

Monday 20 April

Very fine. Rode to Winchcomb, passing by Southam, the ancient seat of the Delabere family. Having ordered my dinner walked to Sudeley Castle, the property of Lord Rivers. Finely situated on a gentle eminence, though surrounded and commanded on each side by hills. The effect of the ruins is much injured by the massive buildings annexed and adjoining them, viz the old mansion house and the barn which, if removed, the ruinous group of buildings would have a beautiful effect, being very advantagiously placed on an isolated knoll.

Their architecture does not bespeak a very early date, being of broad Gothic. The outside shell of the elegant little chapel remains entire, its effect rendered less picturesque by the fruit trees which are trained up against its walls . . . The village of Winchcomb in many points of view presents itself as a picturesque object, though the interior of it bears a melancholy appearance. The church is a handsome building . . .

On my return home I stopt at the summit of the hill to enjoy one of the finest views imaginable. I doubt if England affords a superior. The eye comprehends in one point of view the whole vale from Gloucester to Worcester, in the centre Tewkesbury backed by the Malvern Hills. The Severn appears and disappears in different parts of this rich landscape. The Sugar Loaf and Blorench [*Blorenge*] Hills near Abergavenny are distinctly seen. Numerous churches and other buildings are dispersed over the plain, and the country so richly cultivated and well wooded that scarcely a barren spot is visible through this extensive scenery. The effect was much heightened by the setting sun, partly obscured by clouds and causing some fine partial lights.

Monday 11 May

Left Cheltenham and breakfasted at Winchcomb. Consists chiefly of one long winding street. Many of the houses by their irregular and mixed architecture denote the antiquity of the place. . . . Having taken views of it I proceeded on my journey to Hayles Abbey on a bad, rough horse road. The ruins remaining are trifling, but from their scattered parts and foundations we may conclude this abbey was very extensive. I was informed that the body of the church stood in a meadow between the present chapel and an old tower which is evidently of a much more modern date than the adjoining ruins of the abbey. . . .

Turned off on the right to see Toddington, an old mansion of the Tracy family, now the property of Mr Hanbury, a family from Pontypool in Monmouthshire . . . An old-fashioned house presenting a greater abundance of gable roofs than any house I ever saw. Commanding no good qualities in its situation. Improvements both in the grounds and to the house have been making, but the work advances slowly. Indeed I cannot fancy any person accustomed to the beauties of Monmouthshire settling himself contentedly at Toddington.

Between Hayles Abbey and Toddington saw a double plough at work with six horses and the same number to a single one. The man who held the latter told me that the double one was lately come down for an experiment but he did not think it could answer. Land deep and heavy. Large common fields. Beans, peas, tares etc.

Colt Hoare was wrong in referring to the canal outside Cirencester as the Stroud Navigation. He was looking at the Thames and Severn Canal only a year after the construction had been completed. As for Toddington, the improvements to the house were well worth waiting for, Charles Hanbury-Tracy spending more than £150,000 between 1820 and 1835 in creating the gothic palace that can be seen there today.

In 1802 one Don Manuel Alvarez Espriella made a short journey across the Cotswolds, and his account is published in LETTERS FROM ENGLAND. *Don Manuel is better known to us as Robert Southey, and his book, purporting to be 'translated from the Spanish', was soon exposed as a hoax.*

The Rollright Stones

Stow-on-the-Wold

Tuesday 6 July 1802

We rose at a wholesome hour and were ready before six, when the coach came up. The morning was fine, and we mounted the roof. The country is uninteresting, hills of neither magnitude nor beauty, and fields intersected by stone walls. We passed through a town called Chipping Norton, which stands on the side of a hill, and then descended into a marsh, from whence the little town on the hill side became a fine object.

A few miles beyond, a pillar has been erected to mark the spot where the four shires of Oxford, Warwick, Worcester, and Gloucester meet; this latter one we now entered. Breakfast was ready for us at Moreton-in-Marsh, a place which seems to have little else to support it than its situation on the high road from Worcester to London. Before we entered, the coachman pointed out to us the town of Stow-on-the-Wold, built on a high hill to our left, where he told us there was neither fire, water, nor earth. Water was formerly raised from a deep well by means of a horizontal windmill, but this has fallen to decay.

The marsh ended at Moreton, and we entered upon a country of better features. We crossed the Campden Hills, ascending a long hill from Moreton, travelling about two leagues on the top, and descending to a little town called Broadway. From the height we overlooked the Vale of Evesham, or of the Red Horse, so called from the figure of a horse cut in the side of a hill where the soil is of that colour. . . .

One major source for Cotswold images is the collection of diaries of the Rev. F.E. Witts, written in some ninety notebooks between 1820 and 1852. Witts was rector of Upper Slaughter and had interests on many committees. He was a magistrate who sat regularly at the Quarter Sessions in Gloucester, chairman of the board of guardians for Stow district, a trustee and manager of Stow Provident Bank – and a meticulous observer of life.

21 August 1820

We left home on a tour, with Mrs. Backhouse, who wished by the way to look for a house for her future residence at Gloucester. Her carriage and horses were our mode of conveyance and soon brought us to Frogmill, 10 miles distance, where we baited, and in two hours reached Gloucester, 12 miles further. We went to the King's Head Inn: looked round the town, the spa and its new buildings, visited the County Hall and Gaol.

At the latter I had an interview with Joseph Palmer, a sheep stealer, whom I had committed and who had been tried, sentenced and left for execution. Though found guilty on the clearest and most direct evidence, this hardened young man persisted in denying his crime, at the same time that he had every reason to believe that he would be hanged on the following Saturday: nor did my admonitions appear to affect him more than other exhortations which had been addressed to him.

An exact contemporary of Witts, but one who observed the Cotswolds with an incomparably more experienced, pragmatic and worldly-wise eye was William Cobbett (1763–1835), the journalist and social reformer whose RURAL RIDES, published in 1830, give a compelling and vibrant account of day-to-day life in England in the last years of the Hanoverians. It is interesting to read their works side by side, not merely for the comical effect of their wildly divergent views on, say, the Three Choirs Festival, but for their chronicling of a rural class system that remains, in a less dramatic form, to this day.

First to Cobbett, still seething after a distressing ride north-wards from Swindon:

Cirencester
Wednesday (noon) 7 November 1821.

I slept at a dairy-farm house at Hannington, about eight miles from Swindon, and five on one side of my road. I passed through that villainous hole, Cricklade, about two hours ago; and, certainly, a more rascally looking place I never set my eyes on. I wished to avoid it, but could get along no other way. All along here the land is a whitish stiff loam upon a bed of soft stone, which is found at various distances from the surface, sometimes two feet and sometimes ten. Here and there a field is fenced with this stone, laid together in walls without mortar or earth.

All the houses and out-houses are made of it, and even covered with the thinnest of it formed into tiles. The stiles in the fields are made of large flags of this stone, and the gaps in the hedges are stopped with them – there is very little wood all along here.

The labourers seem miserably poor. Their dwellings are little better than pig-beds, and their looks indicate that their food is not nearly equal to that of a pig. Their wretched hovels are struck upon little bits of ground *on the road side*, where the space has been wider that the road demanded. In many places they have not two rods to a hovel. It seems as if they had been swept off the fields by a hurricane, and had dropped and found shelter under the banks on the road side!

Yesterday morning was a sharp frost; and this had set the poor creatures to digging up their little plots of potatoes. In my whole life I never saw human wretchedness equal to this: no, not even amongst the free negroes in America, who, on an average, do not work one day out of four. And this is '*Prosperity*', is it? These, O Pitt! are the fruits of thy hellish system! However, this *Wiltshire* is a horrible county. This is the county that the *Gallon-loaf* man belongs to. The land all along here is good. Fine fields and pastures all around; and yet the cultivators of those fields so miserable!

This is particularly the case on both sides of Cricklade, and in it too, where everything had the air of the most deplorable want. They are sowing wheat all the way from the Wiltshire downs to Cirencester; though there is some wheat up. Winter vetches are up in some places, and look very well. The turnips of both kinds are good all along here. I met a farmer going with porkers to Highworth market. They would weigh, he said, four score and a half, and he expected to get 7*s*. 6*d*. a score. I expect he will not.

He said they had been fed on barley-meal; but I did not believe him. I put it to his honour, whether whey and beans had not been their food. He looked surly, and pushed on. On this stiff ground, they grow a good many beans, and give them to the pigs with whey; which makes excellent pork for the *Londoners*; but which must meet with a pretty hungry stomach to swallow it in Hampshire.

Gloucester
Thursday (morning) 8 November 1821.

In leaving Cirencester, which is a pretty large town, a pretty nice town, and which the people call *Cititer*, I came up hill into a country, apparently formerly a down or common, but now divided into large fields by stone walls. Anything so ugly I have never seen before. The stone, which, on the other side of Cirencester, lay a good way under ground, here lies very near to the surface. The plough is continually bringing it up, and thus, in general, comes the means of making the walls that serve as fences.

Anything quite so cheerless as this I do not recollect to have seen; for the Bagshot country, and the commons between Farnham and Haslemere, have *heath* at any rate; but these stones are quite abominable. The turnips are not a *fiftieth* of a crop like those of Mr. Clarke at Bergh-Apton in Norfolk, or Mr. Pym at Reygate in Surrey, or of Mr. Brazier at Worth in Sussex. I see thirty acres here that have less *food* upon them than I saw the other day, upon half an acre at Mr. Budd's at Berghclere. *Can* it be good farming to plough and sow and hoe thirty acres to get what *may* be got upon half an acre? Can that half acre cost more than a tenth part as much as the thirty acres?

Little Tew

Condicote

But, if I were to go to this thirty-acre farmer, and tell him what to do to the half-acre, would he not exclaim with the farmer at Botley: "What! *drow* away all that 'ere ground between the *lains!* Jod's blood!"

With the exception of a little dell about eight miles from Cititer, this miserable country continued to the distance of ten miles, when, all of a sudden, I looked down from the top of a high hill into *the vale of Gloucester!* Never was

there, surely, such a contrast in this world! This hill is called *Burlip Hill*; [*Birdlip*] It is much about a mile down it, and the descent so steep as to require the wheel of the chaise to be locked; and, even with that precaution, I did not think it over and above safe to sit in the chaise; so, upon Sir Robert Wilson's principle of taking care of *Number One*, I got out and walked down.

From this hill you see the Morvan Hills in Wales. You

look down into a sort of *dish*, and the City of Gloucester, which you plainly see, at seven miles distance from Burlip Hill, appears to be not far from the centre of the dish. All here is fine; fine farms; fine pastures; all inclosed fields; all divided by hedges; orchards a plenty; and I had scarcely seen one apple since I left Berkshire. Gloucester is a fine, clean, beautiful place; and, which is of a vast deal more importance, the labourers' dwellings, as I came along, looked good, and the labourers themselves pretty well as to dress and healthiness. The girls at work in the fields (always my standard) are not in rags, with bits of shoes tied on their feet and rags tied round their ankles, as they had in Wiltshire.

Oxford
Saturday 17 November 1821.

We . . . took the Hereford coach as it passed through Gloucester, Cheltenham, Northleach, Burford, Whitney [*Witney*], and on to this city, where we arrived about ten o'clock. . . . At *Gloucester* (as there were no meals on the road) we furnished ourselves with nuts and apples, which, first a handful of nuts and then an apple, are, I can assure the reader, excellent and most wholesome fare . . .

From *Gloucester* to *Cheltenham* the country is level, and the land rich and good. The fields along here are ploughed in ridges about 20 feet wide, and the angle of this species of *roof* is pretty nearly as sharp as that of some slated roofs of houses. There is no wet under; it is the top wet only that they aim at keeping from doing mischief.

Cheltenham is a nasty, ill-looking place, half clown and half cockney. The town is one street about a mile long; but then, at some distance from this street, there are rows of white tenements, with green balconies, like those inhabited by the tax-eaters round London. Indeed, this place appears to be the residence of an assemblage of tax-eaters. These vermin shift about between London, Cheltenham,

Relaxation after work

Coln St. Aldwyn

Bath, Bognor, Tunbridge, Ramsgate, Margate, Worthing, and other spots in England, while some of them get over to France and Italy: just like those body-vermin of different sorts, that are found in different parts of the tormented carcasses at different hours of the day and night, and in different degrees of heat and cold.

Cheltenham is at the foot of a part of that chain of hills, which form the sides of that *dish* which I described as resembling the vale of Gloucester. Soon after quitting this resort of the lame and the lazy, the gormandising and guzzling, the bilious and the nervous, we proceeded on, between stone walls, over a country little better than that from Cirencester to Burlip Hill. A very poor, dull, and uninteresting country all the way to Oxford.

Back to Witts, and a 'melancholy accident' that befell one of his dining companions. We wonder what kind of stern moralising on the evils of drink would have ensued if the body in the road had been one of the undeserving poor:

31 March 1824

I proceeded to Gloucester. The forenoon was mostly taken up by me in seeing servants of different descriptions enquiring for places in our family, a quarrel in our kitchen having caused us to dismiss most of our domestics.

The Commission of Assize for the County was opened this afternoon. The new High Sheriff is my friend Thomas John Lloyd-Baker, of Hardwicke Court, a very worthy, intelligent country gentleman and magistrate whose deserved popularity was sufficiently evinced by the very numerous party upwards of 70 gentlemen who dined with him. The hilarity of the evening was, however, exchanged for a strong feeling of gloom by a melancholy accident which befell Mr. Winchcomb Hicks of Eastington, an eminent young clothier and esteemed magistrate, as he was setting out to ride home about 9 o'clock. Though he

appeared quite sober when he left the party, the outward air had the effect of making him very unsteady, insomuch that he was found on the Bristol road, a little beyond the Spa, fallen from his horse and almost dead.

13 June 1825

I left Cheltenham at about 2.30 o'clock. I set off by the Bath and Birmingham coach, being seated on the box. The day, as the preceding had been, was oppressively hot and scorching with no breath of air stirring. Our route was by Stroud and a new line through Painswick. It is a most strikingly beautiful drive . . . fine beech woods clothing the steep knolls, with the road elegantly winding according to the conformation of the side of the hill. Well might the old King exclaim, as it is said he did, surely a finer prospect cannot be seen within my dominions. Prinknash Park, the seat of my friend T. Howell, is a pleasing object adjacent to the road. The venerable old-fashioned mansion, within which I have enjoyed the hospitality of its talented owner, resembles Stanway House in its arrangements and architecture, and like it was of ecclesiastical origin. Mr. Howell's father was editor of the *State Trials*, and the same valuable publication is continued by his son, who was like his father bred to the bar, at which however he does not practise; but at present holds the important situation of Judge Advocate at Gibraltar. While resident on his estate he was an ornament of the bench of magistrates, his legal acquirements being very extensive to which he adds considerable literary acquirements, with a great store of anecdote, and a felicity of expression which renders him a peculiarly agreeable companion.

At Castle Godwin, a small place perched among the beech woods contiguous to Painswick, resides Mr. Lake, formerly of Liverpool, an opulent merchant largely engaged in the silk trade. The situation of Painswick is delightful; this town is in the clothing district.

The living is valuable and in the gift of the inhabitant house-holders of all classes, even the poorest, and consequently elective. On a recent occasion the place presented all the intrigue, bustle and chicanery of a contested borough; legal assessors, counsel and attorneys, bribery, bold swearing, clamour and warm excitement.

At Stroud we found a company of the 10th Hussars: these troops had been summoned a few days ago to assist the civil power in quelling a riotous uprising of the operative weavers. A certain degree of dissatisfaction has existed for some time about wages, which led to disorderly assemblages, actual violence and alarming tumult.

Witts was alluding to the weavers' strike of 1825. There was great hardship and something approaching starvation among many self-employed weavers who worked at their looms at home

John Brinkworth, hedger and ditcher

Yanworth

on an out-work basis for the clothiers of the Stroudwater, Dursley and Wotton valleys. Perhaps the hardest-hit community was Uley, where hundreds of men lost work when Shepherd's Mill went bankrupt in 1826.

W.A. Miles, writing some fourteen years later, gives a graphic account of the 1825 strike in his REPORT AND CONDITION OF THE HAND LOOM WEAVERS OF GLOUCESTERSHIRE:

Many outdoor weavers cannot afford to taste meat; many cannot have tea for breakfast. That meal consists of bread and water with a little salt; it is called 'Tea-kettle Tea'. A journeyman weaver named William Evans states that 'breakfast is warm water with a little salt or some pepper in it, and a crust of bread – but he cannot have enough of that at times.' The dinner of a weaver is generally a piece of bread and cheese, or some potatoes for himself and family, with some fat or 'flick' poured over them. . .

The turnpike road to which Witts referred was the new road from Cheltenham to Stroud through Painswick, noted in the Gloucester Journal of 23 October 1820 by the following passage:

A Correspondent requests us to state that the New Road from Stroud to Cheltenham through Painswick, being completed to Prinknash Park, was opened on the 1st of August by the Commissioners, who afterwards sat down to a sumptuous repast at the Falcon Inn, Painswick; and on the following day, upwards of 100 of the Contractor's workmen were regaled with a dinner at the Bell Inn. The remaining part of the road was let on the 5th of Aug. to Mr. C. Kemp, to whom great credit is due for the masterly way in which the work has been already carried on, and the good conduct and orderly behaviour of his men.

But back to Witts and the weavers:

13 January 1826

The business in hand at the Sessions was the trial of several weavers who, acting under the delusion so prevalent in all manufacturing districts, have been guilty of very serious riots and acts of disturbance at Wotton-under-Edge and its neighbourhood some weeks ago. They proceeded to great violence, assaulting the operatives who undertook work at a lower rate than was approved by them, proceeding to the demolition of workshops and factories, meeting in large companies and debating in their clubs measures to obtain higher wages and control over their masters.

Of these misguided men several were of very decent appearance; one had been a serjeant and enjoyed a pension. They must be punished with severity since the indulgence shown to the Stroud rioters has failed in its effect. The worst cases now will receive two years incarceration in one of the Houses of Correction.

W. A. Miles, in his report on weavers' conditions, put this in perspective when he published in full this letter addressed to him, along with other evidence:

Honourable Sir,

I have worked for my employer, a manufacturer, upwards of seven years. I like them very well in respect of civility. For the first six months I worked on white work, but ever since I have worked on coloured, with a few exceptions; for two years I and my children earned from 16s. to 20s. a week, but since that time it has been getting worse. Our wages were reduced, and we struck for more and accomplished our designs thus far; but we did not keep our price long on account of the multitude of hands and shortness of trade; consequently what we received £2 for we now receive 1s 8d.

Our hours for work are thirteen per day, and we work very hard, as I think some do not *let* more than half-an-hour a day. I earn now from 10s. to 10s. 6d. per week; I think my wife gets 2s. a-week, and I believe my children do not get 6d. per week. I do not expect to get 10s. a-week for the future, as our wages are so very low now. The reason why my children do not earn more is because our abb is spun on *bobbins*, which prevents them from earning at the present time 5s. a-week.

I have a wife, and eight children, and myself, which makes ten in family. I have 12s. 6d. brought in to maintain this family, and to pay other expenses, such as —

	Per Week.	
	s.	d.
House-rent	1	2
Coals, candles and soap	2	6
Poor-rates	0	3
Making	3	11

besides many other little things, leaving only 8s. 7d. to provide food and raiment. Now 8s. 8d. will buy thirteen quarterns of bread, which is five pounds three ounces of bread for each per week, and nothing else.

I am brought so weak that I am not able to work as I was two years ago. I and my children are very destitute of clothes. The Word of God tells me to provide things honest in the sight of men, but I cannot do it; it also tells me I shall get my bread by the sweat of my brow. But I have the sweat of my brow and not the bread, and all through oppression. All that we, as Englishmen, want is plenty of labour, and that which sweetens labour. I have four miles a-day to walk to my work.

I remain, Sir,
Your obedient Servant
George Risby

Erasmus Charlton, Police Sergeant, at Hampton, formerly in the London Police, says of his own personal knowledge that:

The weavers are much distressed: they are wretchedly off in bedding; has seen many cases where the man and his wife and as many as 7 children have slept on straw, laid on the floor with only a torn quilt to cover them; sometimes he has had occasion to search the houses of some weavers on suspicion of stolen yarn or slinge, and has witnessed very distressing cases; children crying for food, and the parents having neither food nor money in the house, or work to obtain any; he has frequently given them money out of his own pocket to provide them with a breakfast.

These men have a great dread of going to the Poor House, and live in constant hope that every day will bring them some work; witness has frequently told them they would be better in the house, and their answer has been '*We would rather starve.*' Considers this wretched state stints the children in growth, and causes a deal of sickness; does not think that one family out of 10, children and adults, can attend the church, in consequence of their ragged condition; has often dropped in at meal times and found them eating potatoes with a bit of flick or suet.

In reference to wages it has been stated to witness by shop-loom weavers, that in the factory, as the work is confined to one individual, the power of increasing his earnings by means of the wife and children's labour is diminished.

The habits of a weaver are not settled or industrious like the agricultural labourer; and that if they were in good work, they would want to play one or two days out of the six.

Cobbett, too, was all too aware of 'poor creatures . . . living upon potatoes', this time the agricultural labourers whose long hours of effort helped boost someone else's bank balance:

Westonbirt

Lower Slaughter

Malmesbury
Monday 11 September 1826.

I was detained at Highworth partly by the rain and partly by Company that I liked very much. I left it at six o'clock yesterday morning, and got to this town about three or four o'clock in the afternoon, after a ride, including my deviations, of 34 miles; and as pleasant a ride as man ever had. I got to a farm-house in the neighbourhood of Cricklade to breakfast, at which house I was very near to the source of the river Isis, which is, they say, the first branch of the Thames. They call it the 'Old Thames', and I rode through it here, it not being above four or five yards wide, and not deeper than the knees of my horse.

The land here, and all round Cricklade, is very fine. Here are some of the very finest pastures in all England, and some of the finest dairies of cows, from 40 to 60 in a dairy, grazing in them. Was not this *always* so? Was it created by the union with Scotland; or was it begotten by Pitt and his crew? Aye, it was always so; and there were formerly two churches here, where there is now only one, and five, six, or ten times as many people.

I saw in one single farm-yard here more food than enough for four times the inhabitants of the parish; and this yard did not contain a tenth, perhaps, of the produce of the parish; but while the poor creatures that raise the wheat and the barley and cheese and the mutton and the beef are living upon potatoes, an accursed *canal* comes kindly through the parish to convey away the wheat and all the good food to the tax-eaters and their attendants in the Wen!

What, then, is this 'an improvement?' Is a nation *richer* for the carrying away of the food from those who raise it, and giving it to bayonet men and others, who are assembled in great masses? I could broom-stick the fellow who would look me in the face and call this 'an improvement.' What! was it not better for the consumers of the food to live near to the places where it was grown?

We have very nearly come to the system of Hindostan, where the farmer is allowed by the *Aumil*, or tax collector, only so much of the produce of his farm to eat in the year! The thing is not done in so undisguised a manner here: here are assessor, collector, exciseman, supervisor, informer, constable, justice, sheriff, jailer, judge, jury, jack-ketch, barrack-man. Here is a great deal of ceremony about it; all is done according to law; it is the *free-est* country in the world: but, somehow or other, the produce is, at last, *carried away*; and it is eaten, for the main part, by those who do not work. . . .

When I got in here yesterday, I went, at first, to an inn; but I very soon changed my quarters for the house of a friend, who and whose family, though I had never seen them before, and had never heard of them until I was at Highworth, gave me a hearty reception, and precisely in *the style* that I like.

This town, though it has nothing particularly engaging in itself, stands upon one of the prettiest spots that can be imagined. Besides the river Avon, which I went down in the south-east part of the country, here is another river Avon, which runs down to Bath, and two branches, or sources, of which meet here. There is a pretty ridge of ground, the base of which is a mile or a mile and a half wide. On each side of this ridge a branch of the river runs down, through a flat of very fine meadows.

The town and the beautiful remains of the famous old abbey stand on the rounded spot which terminates this ridge; and, just below, nearly close to the town, the two branches of the river meet; and then they begin to be called *the Avon*. The land round about is excellent, and of a great variety of forms. The trees are lofty and fine: so that what with the water, the meadows, the fine cattle and sheep, and, as I hear, the absence of *hard*-pinching poverty, this is a very pleasant place.

There remains more of the abbey than, I believe, of any

of our monastic buildings, except that of Westminster, and those that have become cathedrals. The church service is performed in the part of the abbey that is left standing. The parish church has fallen down and is gone; but the tower remains, which is made use of for the bells; but the abbey is used as the church, though the church-tower is at a considerable distance from it. It was once a most magnificent building; and there is now a *doorway* which is the most beautiful thing I ever saw, and which was, nevertheless, built in Saxon times, in 'the *dark* ages,' and was built by men who were not begotten by Pitt nor by Jubilee George. What *fools*, as well as ungrateful creatures, we have been and are!

There is a broken arch, standing off from the sound part of the building, at which one cannot look up without feeling shame at the thought of ever having abused the men who made it. No one need *tell* any man of sense; he *feels* our inferiority to our fathers upon merely beholding the remains of their efforts to ornament their country and elevate the minds of the people . . .

There is a *market-cross* in this town, the sight of which is worth a journey of hundreds of miles. Time, with his scythe, and 'enlightened Protestant piety', with its pick-axes and crow-bars; these united have done much to efface the beauties of this monument of ancient skill and taste, and proof of ancient wealth; but in spite of all their destructive efforts this cross still remains a most beautiful thing, though possibly, and even probably, nearly, or quite, a thousand years old.

There is a *market-cross* lately erected at Devizes, and intended to imitate the ancient ones. Compare that with this, and then you have, pretty fairly, a view of the difference between us and our forefathers of the 'dark-ages.'

To-morrow I start for Bollitree, near Ross, Here-fordshire, my road being across the county, and through the city of Gloucester.

Stroud
Tuesday Forenoon, 12 September 1826.

I set off from Malmesbury this morning at 6 o'clock, in as sweet and bright a morning as ever came out of the heavens, and leaving behind me as pleasant a house and as kind hosts as I ever met with in the whole course of my life, either in England or America; and that is saying a great deal indeed. This circumstance was the more pleasant, as I had never before either seen or heard of these kind, unaffected, sensible, *sans-facons*, and most agreeable friends.

From Malmesbury I first came, at the end of five miles, to Tutbury, [*Tetbury*] which is in Gloucestershire, there being here a sort of dell, or ravine, which in this place, is a boundary line of the two counties, and over which you go on a bridge, one-half of which belongs to each county . . .

A little way before I got to Tutbury I saw a woman digging some potatoes in a strip of ground making part of a field nearly an oblong square, and which field appeared to be laid out in strips. She told me that the field was part of a farm (to the homestead of which she pointed); that it was, by the farmer, *let out* in strips to labouring people; that each strip contained a rood (or quarter of a statute acre); that each married labourer rented one strip; and that the annual rent was *a pound* for the strip.

Now the taxes being all paid by the farmer; the fences being kept in repair by him; and, as appeared to me, the land being exceedingly good: all these things considered, the rent does not appear to be too high. This fashion is certainly a *growing* one; it is a little step towards a coming back to the ancient small life and leaseholds and common-fields! This field of strips was, in fact, a sort of common-field; and the 'agriculturists,' as the conceited asses of landlords call themselves, at their clubs and meetings, might, and they would if their skulls could admit any thoughts except such as relate to high prices and low

Chedworth

Hampnett

wages; they might, and they would, begin to suspect that the 'dark age' people were not so very foolish when they had so many common-fields, and when almost every man that had a family had also a bit of land, either large or small.

Just before I got into Tutbury I was met by a good many people, in twos, threes, or fives, some running, and some walking fast, one of the first of whom asked me if I had met an 'old man' some distance back. I asked what *sort* of a man.

'A *poor* man.'

'I don't recollect, indeed; but what are you all pursuing him for?'

'Cabbages.'

'Where?'

'Out of Mr. Glover, the hatter's garden.'

'What! do you call that *stealing*; and would you punish a man, a poor man, and therefore, in all likelihood, a hungry man too, and moreover an old man; do you set up a hue-and-cry after, and would you punish, such a man for taking a few cabbages, when the Holy Bible, which, I dare say, you profess to believe in, and perhaps assist to circulate, teaches you that the hungry man may, without committing any offence at all, go into his neighbour's vineyard and eat his fill of grapes, one bunch of which is worth a sack-full of cabbages?'

'Yes; but he is a very bad character.'

'Why, my friend, very poor and almost starved people are apt to be "bad characters;" but the Bible, in both Testaments, commands us to be merciful to the poor, to feed the hungry, to have compassion on the aged; and it makes no exception as to the "character" of the parties.'

Another group or two of the pursuers had come up by this time; and I, bearing in mind the fate of Don Quixote when he interfered in somewhat similar cases, gave my horse the hint, and soon got away; but though doubtless I made no converts, I, upon looking back, perceived that I had slackened the pursuit! The pursuers went more slowly; I could see that they got to talking; it was now the step of deliberation rather than that of decision; and though I did not like to call upon Mr. Glover, I hope he was merciful.

It is impossible for me to witness scenes like this; to hear a man called *a thief* for such a cause; to see him thus eagerly and vindictively pursued for having taken some cabbages in a garden: it is impossible for me to behold such a scene, without calling to mind the practice in the United States of America, where, if a man were even to talk of prosecuting another (especially if that other were poor or old) for taking from the land, or from the trees, any part of a growing crop, for his own personal and immediate use . . . such talker would be held in universal abhorrence . . .

Tutbury is a very pretty town, and has a beautiful ancient church. The country is high along here for a mile or two towards Avening, which begins a long and deep and narrow valley, that comes all the way down to Stroud. When I got to the end of the high country, and the lower country opened to my view, I was about three miles from Tutbury, on the road to Avening, leaving the Minchinhampton road to my right. Here I was upon the edge of the high land, looking right down upon the village of Avening, and seeing, just close to it, a large and fine mansion house, a beautiful park, and, making part of the park, one of the finest, most magnificent woods (of 200 acres, I dare say), lying facing me, going from a valley up a gently rising hill.

While I was sitting on my horse, admiring this spot, a man came along with some tools in his hand, as if going somewhere to work as a plumber. 'Whose beautiful place is that?' said I.

'One Squire Ricardo, I think they call him, but . . . '

You might have knocked me down with a feather, as the old women say . . .

'But' (continued the plumber) 'the Old Gentleman's

dead, and . . .'

'God —, the old gentleman and the young gentleman too!' said I, and giving my horse a blow instead of a word, on I went down the hill.

Before I got to the bottom, my reflections on the present state of the 'market' and on the probable results of 'watching the turn of it' had made me better humoured; and as one of the first objects that struck my eye in the village was the sign of the Cross, and of the Red, or Bloody, Cross too, I asked the landlord some questions, which began a series of joking and bantering that I had with the people, from one end of the village to the other. I set them all a laughing; and though they could not know my name, they will remember me for a long while.

This estate of Gatcombe belonged, I am told, to a Mr. Shepperd, and to his fathers before him. I asked where this

Upper Slaughter

Nailsworth

Shepperd was now? A tradesman-looking man told me that he did not know where he was; but that he had heard that he was living somewhere near to Bath! Thus they go! Thus they are squeezed out of existence. The little ones are gone; and the big ones have nothing left for it but to resort to the bands of holy matrimony with the turn of the market watchers and their breed. This the big ones are now doing apace; and there is comfort at any rate; namely that the connection cannot make them baser than they are, a boroughmonger being, of all God's creatures, the very basest.

From Avening I came on through Nailsworth, Woodchester, and Rodborough to this place. These villages lie on the sides of a narrow and deep valley, with a narrow stream of water running down the middle of it, and this stream turns the wheels of a great many mills and sets of machinery for the making of *woollen-cloth*.

The factories begin at Avening, and are scattered all the way down the valley. There are steam-engines as well as water powers. The work and the trade is so flat that in, I should think, much more than a hundred acres of ground, which I have seen today, covered with rails or racks, for the drying of cloth, I do not think that I have seen one single acre where the racks had cloth upon them. The workmen do not get half wages; great numbers are thrown on the parish; but overseers and magistrates in this part of England do not presume that they are to leave anybody to starve to death; there is law here; this is in England, and not in 'the North,' where those who ought to see that the poor do not suffer talk of their dying with hunger as Irish squires do; aye, and applaud them for their patient resignation!

The Gloucestershire people have no notion of dying with hunger; and it is with great pleasure that I remark that I have seen no woe-worn creature this day. The sub-soil here is a yellowish ugly stone. The houses are all built with this; and it being ugly, the stone is made *white* by a wash of

some sort or other. The land on both sides of the valley, and all down the bottom of it, has plenty of trees on it; it is chiefly pasture land, so that the green and the white colours, and the form and great variety of the ground, and the water, altogether make this a very pretty ride.

Here are a series of spots, every one of which a lover of landscapes would like to have painted. Even the buildings of the factories are not ugly. The people seem to have been constantly well off. A pig in almost every cottage sty; that is the infallible mark of a happy people. At present this valley suffers; and though cloth will always be wanted, there will yet be much suffering even here, while at Uly and other places they say the suffering is great indeed.

Huntley
Between Gloucester and Ross.

From Stroud I came up to Pitchcomb, leaving Painswick on my right. From the lofty hill at Pitchcomb I looked down into that great flat and almost circular vale, of which the city of Gloucester is in the centre. To the left I saw the Severn become a sort of arm of the sea; and before me I saw the hills that divide this county from Herefordshire and Worcestershire. The hill is a mile down. When down, you are amongst dairy-farms and orchards all the way to Gloucester, and, this year, the orchards, particularly those of pears, are very productive. I intended to sleep at Gloucester, as I had, when there, already come twenty-five miles, and as the fourteen, which remained for me to go, in order to reach Bollitree, in Herefordshire, would make about nine more than either I or my horse had a taste for.

But when I came to Gloucester, I found that I should run a risk of having no bed if I did not bow very low and pay very high; for what should there be here, but one of those scandalous and beastly fruits of the system, called a 'music-meeting!' Those who founded the cathedrals never

dreamed, I dare say, that they would have been put to such uses as this! They are, upon these occasions, made use of as *Opera Houses*; and I am told that the money which is collected goes, in some shape or another, to the clergy of the church, or their widows, or children, or something.

These assemblages of player-folks, half-rogues and half-fools, began with the small paper-money; and with it they will go. They are amongst the profligate pranks which

idleness plays when fed by the sweat of a starving people. From this scene of prostitution and of pocket-picking I moved off with all convenient speed, but not before the ostler made me pay 9*d*. for merely letting my horse *stand* about ten minutes, and not before he had *begun* to abuse me for declining, though in a very polite manner, to make him a present in addition to the 9*d*. How he ended I do not know; for I soon set the noise of the shoes of my horse to

The village smithy, Kingham

Shearing by hand

answer him. I got to this village about half-past seven, and I am going to bed with an intention of getting to Bollitree (six miles only) early enough in the morning to catch my sons in bed if they play the sluggard.

The old radical was disappointed in trying to catch his sons in bed. He met his son Richard on the road to Bollitree, and Richard had already been up an hour. Earlier, at Gatcombe Park, now the Princess Royal and Captain Mark Phillips's home, Cobbett could not resist a posthumous dig at an old adversary – David Ricardo M.P., a political economist with distinct establishment leanings, who had died three years earlier.

The house was built by the clothier Edward Sheppard in around 1770, and after buying it from his son in 1814 Ricardo altered it considerably in the brief time before his death at the age of 51.

Cobbett's distaste for the Three Choirs Festival was not shared by Francis Witts. The diarist was in Gloucester on the same day, and recorded the festivities from a very different perspective:

13 September 1826

The town was all alive with company, some crowding towards the college, some arriving at the inns and lodgings, all in gay attire, and nothing could be more lovely than the weather. A large posse of constables under the able generalship of a Bow Street Officer was posted at the Cathedral door, and their services were likely to be needed for the admission this morning was free.

Each Steward's share of tickets for the galleries was 25, and the lay and clerical galleries held about 60 persons and were each day almost exclusively occupied by the first ladies in point of rank and connection, who attended the meeting, a most beautiful sight and the present style of female dress tended to justify the appellations affixed, a parterre – a bed of roses. My own ladies were each day accommodated in the first row of the clerical gallery, and

from the extent of my acquaintance I was each morning soon drained of my tickets, and had I twice as many could have disposed of them to various applicants.

By 11 o'clock the inner choir of the Cathedral was fearfully crowded . . . an occasional scream or groan indicated distress or fainting, some were carried out, some struggled into the outer choir, the most persevering stood their ground. The whole was opened with Handel's sublime Overture to Esther . . .

The concert at the Shire Hall was very fully attended, nearly a thousand persons were present and the pressure at the upper end of the room very great. Lady Lyttelton and the Misses Witts were there, and as soon as I had provided for their accommodation by a fresh bench between those already occupied and the orchestra, the well-known and obtrusive Alderman Matthew Wood of London, coveting similar accommodation, addressed himself to me.

I explained it had been the constant rule with the Stewards to reserve accommodation for their own parties, and with very few forms kept back and the Lord Lieutenant not yet arrived he would have to find accommodation in the seats already placed. In reply the Alderman (who since the death of the sister of his namesake, the eccentric and wealthy Jemmy Wood, Banker of Gloucester, has been a summer resident here, where the old lady left him a good house in consideration of his championship of the late Queen Caroline, and where he hopes to worm himself into the good graces of Banker Jemmy) dilated on the ill-usage of the public by the stewards: then exit in a rage.

When the conversation reached the ears of Bowles the following day when we were summing up the receipts at the Cathedral door, the poet extemporised:

What money our music produces;
For surely a meeting is good
Where are Beauforts and Sherbornes and Ducies
And Lansdownes and Alderman Wood.

The receipts for the charity amounted to £816 1*s*. 8*d*.

At the close of the concert I remained an hour assisting in the *devoirs* of the tea rooms, and enjoying while I strolled about with my friend Howell, the profusions of the youthful in merry dance; here a high-born fastidious group in graceful meanders moving in the light quadrille, there a less well-bred but equally well-satisfied dandy, perchance an attorney's clerk, balancing and pointing a fantastic toe, opposite to some rosy good humoured country girl, a belle from Stroud or Tewkesbury.

12 October 1827

I inspected the treadwheel at Northleach Bridewell, recently put up. The machinery still requires some alterations. The velocity with which the wheel revolved was too great, so that the fatigue exceeded the strength of the prisoners. The revolutions should be limited to about 52 steps in a minute. A regulator must be applied to the machine in such a manner as to compensate for any difference in the weight of the gangs on the wheel, whether grown men or boys.

The millwright was in attendance. It is intended to keep the machine going, should there at any time be a failure of corn to grind. Nine or ten prisoners were on the mill at once, they worked each 4½ or 5 minutes, one descending from the extremity of the wheel every half minute. A relay of prisoners is kept in an adjacent yard, walking in a circle.

24 June 1837

A brilliant summer day. My son rode with me to Stow to attend the ceremony of proclaiming Queen Victoria. A subscription having been raised to fee the bell ringers and musicians, a humble procession was got up, headed by the Rector, myself and my son, the clerk proclaiming our Sovereign Lady in four stations, with 'God Save the Queen' by the band, cheers by the crowd, the inner circle being formed by the principal tradesmen. The proclamation overtook luncheon at the Rectory with the Vavasour family.

28 June 1838

A very fine day. Auspicious weather for the Queen's Coronation, which was celebrated generally with great spirit and zeal. Great preparations at Stow for doing the due honour of the day, and an exhibition of loyalty by distribution of the good things of life to the poor, and provide a dinner for 400 in the market place; beef, mutton, beer, etc: I returned home to dinner, and shortly afterwards Margaret and I distributed cake and cheese, and beer to about 40 children of our Free School and Sunday School, and a party of 15 or 16 sat down in my servants' hall to a substantial Coronation supper, the partakers of the good cheer being our servants, hatmakers, labourers, and the masters and mistress of the parish schools. The farmers gave treats to the rest of the villagers.

On this same fine day William Augustus Miles, the chronicler of the weavers' conditions, was walking through the village of Horsley, near Nailsworth:

On the day of the coronation, when the weavers and others were enjoying the holiday, I entered the neatest cottage I ever saw. I was attracted to it by the click of the loom, a sound unusual on a general holiday: the owner of the cottage was in his loom, hard at work.

His house was neat to a degree; he had his small looking glass, or mirror, over a neat mantelpiece, on which were ranged common but well selected ornaments; the clock-case was polished most carefully; the round three-legged table was as white as soap and care could make it, nor was there the slightest indication of slovenly or neglectful habits. Jonathan Cole was the master and owner of this

The Old Elm Tree, Bishop's Cleeve

Monk's Mill, Alderley

cottage: he had always been a weaver since he was 14 or 15, and is now 48 years of age. He was thrifty, had bought his land and built upon it his own house.

The history and evidence of this provident man is best given in his own words.

Jonathan Cole, a weaver at Horsley, states,

That when he earned only 4*s*. a week he contrived, by living upon bread and water, to save 3*d*. one week, but could save no more for a long time; the 'coppers' were cankered before he could put more to them; he heard of a benefit club, but he made his own calculations, and put away as much as if he had subscribed to it, together with the amount which he considered his club would have cost, and called it his *own* club, and in 20 years he saved *a hundred pounds*.

In 1824 he bought a piece of ground to build a small

cottage, but his neighbours persuaded him to build a larger one, to his cost; he did so by borrowing money, and now he has to pay interest, which hurts him. It was built to hold four looms; he cannot now let it: he did once, but did not get paid. His father was a weaver, and taught him, and he went home to work in one of his father's looms, at the age of 17; is now 48 years of age.

Witness states that 31 years ago . . . he was paid . . . 8*s.* 8*d.* a week wages; his lodgings were found for him; paid his mother 3*d.* per week for washing, and he paid for his food. When his savings began he put by 3*d.* a week, and 6*d.* extra when he could; was able, before he built his house, to buy 4 looms, second-hand, one at a time, and yet keep his fund untouched; these looms had pretty constant work for 10 years, and earned him 2*s.* 6*d.* a week each, making 10*s.* a week clear; was married, but had no children; his wife was poorly and earned but little, and cost somewhat in physic.

Witness entered into a furniture club, and got a clock and other furniture: paid 1*s.* per week; lived pretty well; had a joint of meat a week, and some beer in the house; repairs and furniture took a good deal of his money, and he laid out £23 8*s.* to purchase a bit of ground to prevent any one from building near his windows . . . this land now serves him as a garden, and provides garden stuff: owes £140 on mortgage, and £50 on note of hand; probably the place is not worth more than the mortgage.

Ten years ago, when the strike took place, he was persuaded to turn out; was compelled not to take out work at the lower price, and got turned off by his master, who never employed him again, and he has not been able to get regular work since; sometimes only work for one loom, sometimes two, generally stripe-work; has not yet sold any of his looms; cannot get a purchaser for them; made some loss by doing work for a manufacturer who failed and has not paid him.

The wages were lowered to 30*s.* soon after the strike, from 35*s.*, and three or four years ago were lowered to 20*s.*; it is now 18*s.* 8*d.* and glue, and the length, instead of being 28 ells, is 33 ells; could earn, if he had constant work, 9*s.* 4*d.* a-week, hard work, and have to pay out of it quilling and candles; should work from five till eight, or as long as he could see, in the summer, and by candles in the winter, has been at play for weeks at a time; he could just make a bare subsistence.

Could, if he had constant work for two looms, pay his rent or mortgage interest, rates, &c., but, as it is, he is now reduced to a state of great difficulty. If he was called upon to pay all he owes his whole property, at the present prices, would hardly pay his debts, and he should be turned into the streets without the means of providing for himself.

Is now paid in truck at Mr. Webb's, Chalford, and has been for this year past; gets goods enough to maintain himself, and had 4*s.* in money out of two chains: thinks he is served as well at the truck shop as if he bought goods elsewhere.

Witness states that he could get work in a shop-factory if he chose, because he is a steady man, but then his looms and tools would be useless; many of his fellow weavers are on the parish, and there is an allotment of land for every person in distress; knows some weavers have got it, and that it almost maintains them; almost all the neighbours are gone to shop-looms. Witness does not know the cause of the distress, except that there are more hands than can do the work, and does not know a remedy.

It would be interesting to know if this Silas Marner had as happy an ending to his tale as George Eliot manages for her fictional weaver. The truck shop was where the weaver was paid in goods instead of money. The system had been much abused by employers and was illegal by the time Victoria came to the throne, having been banned by Act of Parliament in 1831. Further Acts in 1887 and 1896 were necessary, however, before it was finally stamped out.

Painswick

Hidcot Manor

In 1868 a successful Yorkshire merchant, Dearman Birchall, moved to the edge of the Cotswolds and bought Bowden Hall in Upton St. Leonards. His diary records a county society and local life far removed from what he was used to in Leeds:

20 September 1868

Arrived at Gloucester 4.15 a.m. Sunday. Took the sacrament at the Cathedral, which is newly restored and very pretty. In afternoon to Bowden Hall, Upton St. Leonards, beautiful drive 4 miles. Church and graveyard very pretty. Hall appearing at a distance on the side of a hill surrounded by fine timber, large bow-windowed house. Views of finely timbered fields; *tout ce qu'il y a de beau.*

21 September 1868

Caught 7.40 train to Cirencester. Scenery through Stroudwater Valley exceedingly lovely and apparently undefiled by smoke. Earl Bathurst's Park opposite station at Cirencester has majestic and most glorious timber. The Agricultural College most picturesque Gothic building with broken outline. Mr. Constable and his amiable wife drove me through Stroud to Bowden Hall, calling on Mr. Hyett at Painswick House on our way. We were delighted with Bowden. Mansion with 215 acres, 8 cottages, 2 sets of farm buildings, £2,000 worth of timber, the whole for £25,000. Its proximity to Cheltenham and Gloucester, its church, and the society make me sorely tempted.

Bowden Hall 4 miles from Gloucester and 8 from Cheltenham.

Reasons for. Situation between two desirable places and reasonable distance. Good society and extra good chances of introductions. Agreeable country. Lovely situation and surroundings of the house; to my mind views from the estate are very fine, soil prolific, timber old and handsome, house plain but convenient. Cheltenham affords good masters for Clara and more congenial society for her, and more to my mind than the Tennants and Harrisons who form the children's circle at Scarcroft.

Against. Could not let for 2 years and I am not disposed to leave here (Scarcroft, near Leeds) for at least a year. Charles Brooke Hunt, proprietor, desires to go abroad for a time, and does not accede to my suggestion that he should remain as a tenant for 2 years. My lease of Scarcroft lasts until Oct. 1st 1871 and owing to the badness of trade could not be let at present. Some doubt whether it might be damp from amount of trees and the clay soil which exists in the valley. My new engagements in Leeds make it undesirable I should leave at present – shooting in neighbourhood. A good deal to do at the house, being brick plastered and colour-washed, the windows numerous with old and ugly glass.

Dearman Birchall's reasons for outweighed those against, and he bought Bowden Hall. Clara was his six-year-old daughter, her mother having died shortly after her birth. In October of the following year Dearman had woman problems and servant problems in the same week. The first concerned a certain Miss Somerset:

5 October 1869

. . . The position is embarrassing; her proximity, her constant calls for one object or another, unlimited intercourse without meeting where we could have any prolonged conversation. It is dangerous for one's peace of mind to be much with so sweetly fresh a girl. In her favour are her transparent honesty, off-handedness and sprightliness, love of home and the poor, apparent love to her sisters. Against: parentage means – so much needed by her nearest relatives, her taking possession of us and making so very free, and in the circumstances perhaps we would have admired her more if she had not made herself so cheap, her passion for riding or doing anything and feeling of weariness with inactivity.

Personally I like the girl, but is she what I should desire as a mother for Clara? Is she capable of loving me for my own sake and as warmly if I lived in a cottage, or is Bowden Hall with its reminiscences the bait which allures her? The worst suspicion which can occur, is she playing for the Hall or capable of so base a game?

In this instance the methodical and coolly calculating Dearman's 'against' list won the day. He eventually married Emily Jowitt in 1873, when he was 45 and she just 20.

Back to October 1869, and the servant problems:

Naunton

8 October 1869

Elizabeth [*a maid*] came and complained that Elwood Gell had taken some liberty with her on 14 Sept. She thought he had drunk some beer and had only proceeded as far as giving her a kiss. On Saturday evening he came into the laundry and stood about, someone else being there as well as Elizabeth. When they left he came and threw her on to the ground, got on to her and did his utmost to commit a rape. She wonders now that she had sufficient strength to scream or breathe. William Moulding stood outside looking on, and dare not render any assistance. Elwood said he had set his mark on her and would have her. She is afraid of his taking her life.

On consulting Thomas I found he was convinced that the account given me by Elizabeth was essentially correct. It surprised him the more because Elwood had stood aloof from the servants, never sitting in the kitchen or joking with them. In fact he had invariably conducted himself with the utmost propriety. As Elizabeth had not mentioned this until Thursday, and it occurred last Saturday, and we are engaged to go to the Diocesan Conference tomorrow, I delayed dismissing him until our return.

9 October 1869

Elwood drove us into Gloucester, and while we were at the meeting in the Shire Hall effected some shopping and then drove as far as Capt. Arthur Stewart's (Saintbridge) to meet Clara and Miss Van. They noticed he drove them very wildly to the station, to which place they proceeded to meet the Newloves, who were passing through on their way home.

While there Elwood drove away. He was very drunk, and on getting to the Bell came into collision with a hay cart, bent the lamp and slipped off his box. The head hostler got him into a cab and sent him home, and I drove our party (which included the vicar Mr. Green) from the meeting. When we got to the King's Head (just outside Upton) the cab was standing at the door and Mr. Green kindly volunteered to go in and see Elwood Gell. I also directed the cabman to take him to his cottage.

I forestalled him there and saw his wife, in a few words putting her in possession of the above particulars. She said it was one of the first times he had misconducted himself when out with carriage or horses, but when intoxicated he was a raving lunatic, and he had so ill-treated her on Saturday last that she and her son had spent the night in the fields. His brutality was such she was determined to see him no more, so I sought an asylum for her at George Clapham's, and so when Elwood returned the bird had flown.

10 October 1869

Elwood was apparently very penitent and looked respectable, though sad and depressed. I warned him off the premises. He gave the key of the house to me for his wife, and after trying to induce her to join him he went away. I hear they have £150 in the Bank in Gloucester, the remains of £300 he got with her as a marriage portion, left by a grandmother. I suppose he will bag this and drink it. Mrs. Clapham seems to think Mrs. Gell is now repenting not going with him.

16 October 1869

It appears probable Elwood Gell has taken his departure for America. He drew £95 out of the bank.

Most of Dearman Birchall's diary deals with his social life, dinner parties with county society or rides with the hounds, the Berkeley and the Cotswold. But perhaps his greatest preoccupation was with the Church; he was a close friend of Bishop and Mrs Ellicott and the Dean of Gloucester.

An entry for 1872 reads:

. . . Lunched with the Dean and gave him £100 towards the restoration of the Cathedral. He was very amusing about Mrs. Ellicott, and said she kissed his mastiff dog more heartily than he guessed she ever kissed the Bishop. . .

In an adjoining diocese the Rev. Francis Kilvert did not move in nearly such exalted circles, but for literary style and sheer beauty of writing little can compare with his diaries. He divided his time between Herefordshire and Wiltshire, and did not go out of his way to describe his journeys through Gloucestershire while travelling between the two, but there are still some fascinating glimpses:

Tuesday 11 October 1870

Letters from Emmie, my Father and Dora. I am sorry to hear he was much knocked up after attending the funeral of Aunt Mary at [*South*] Cerney . . .

Visited Edward Evans in the dark hole in the hovel roof which does duty for a bedroom, and a gaunt black and white ghostly cat was stalking about looking as if she were only waiting for the sick man to die, that she might begin upon him.

Dined at Pont Vaen and played Chess with Bridge. Going towards Chain Alley I saw a pair of dark beautiful eyes looking softly and lovingly through the dusk, earnest and eager to be recognized, and the slight delicate girlish figure of the Flower of the Border stood within her grandmother's door, her round olive cheeks shaded by her rich clusters of dark curls.

A happy smile broke over her beautiful face, as she looked up shyly and spoke. When I came back a little before midnight the house was dark, but as I passed under the windows I heard the child's voice speaking in the bedroom. Chain Alley is a dangerous, terrible neighbourhood for a beautiful girl to be reared in. God keep thee my child.

Kilvert, a very close contemporary of his fellow clergyman Lewis Carroll – ALICE'S ADVENTURES IN WONDERLAND was first published in 1865 – shared the writer's preoccupation with pretty young girls, but perhaps we should not take too *cynical a late-twentieth-century view of such relationships. Alice, of 'wonderland' fame was also a Cotswold girl. Her name was Alice Liddell, and her father was the vicar of South Cerney. Kilvert was equally illuminating when recording other aspects of life:*

Monday 10 February 1873

My Mother says that at Dursley in Gloucestershire, when ladies and gentlemen used to go out to dinner together on dark nights, the gentlemen pulled out the tails of their shirts and walked before to show the way and light the ladies. These were called 'Dursley Lanterns'.

Monday 12 October 1874

After school this morning I walked to Malmesbury. It was a lovely autumn day and very warm walking. I left Langley Burrell at 11 o'clock and walking slowly on account of the heat reached Malmesbury about 2 o'clock. I went by Sutton, then by Upper Seagry, Startley and Rodbourne, quite a new road to me.

As I passed by Burton Hill at the entrance into Malmesbury I met a fine handsome old man with a white beard, a labouring man with a spade over his shoulder. He touched his hat and asked if I had preached at the Abbey yesterday. I told him, 'No.'

'Then it was your?' he said. 'It was some one very much like you.'

I asked how the Vicar, Mr. Pitt, was. 'Very ill,' he said, adding, 'His father and my father were brothers' children, but one family has gone up and the other down.' He and the vicar had a common great-grandfather. I asked if the Vicar recognized him. 'No,' he said. He told me he had been footman at Cole Park, pointing to the tops of the elms in the rookery avenue leading to the house, and had often nursed 'the Young Squire', the late Mr. Audley Lovel, who died some years ago at the age of 60 or more.

Bisley

Swan Hotel, Bibury

I went into the Abbey Church, through the grandest Norman doorway in the world, arch within arch sculptured richly with pictured medallions of the history of the Bible.

The mitred Abbot was sitting in state in his box high up on the South wall, ready to bless the people, and the monks walked aloft in solemn silence round the church by the triforium, appearing and disappearing through the narrow arches.

I called on Mrs. Jennings at the Abbot's House. She was at home and very kind, but sweet lovely Maud was away at Shoreham and I was much disappointed. As I sat looking out at the open window northwards toward Tetbury, the window from which the Abbot of Malmesbury must so often have looked, I thought I had seldom so seen a more lovely and peaceful view.

The island city sloped steeply down towards the Westport and the Mill, from which the water, rushing in a cascade with a sweet refreshing sound, came winding in a dark, still, glossy stream round the foot of the steep green mount upon which the grey-buttressed high-gabled Abbot's house is built.

We looked down upon the golden heads of the chestnuts and limes and the reflections of the trees glassed in the quiet water, and beneath the mullioned window a brindled cow and white pony grazed along the side of the steep green knoll that sloped down to the river.

Mrs. Jennings took me out into the garden at my request, by the ancient wooden bolted door and under the beautiful Saxon vandyked arch beneath which the Abbot used to go into the Church by a private entrance. She showed me, too, the sight of King Athelstan's grave near where the High Altar used to stand. An asparagus bed now waves over the spot.

Mrs. Luce of the Knoll (the widow of Captain Luce) came in to call. Mr. Jennings has for some time been looking out for a surgeon's assistant. I was duly introduced. 'Oh,' said Mrs. Luce, 'this is the young man who has just come to help in the surgery.'

'No, no,' explained Mrs. Jennings hastily.

Mrs. Luce then besought me to help her to let her stabling to some hunting man for the winter.

As I went down the steep winding street I met Andrews, the Rector of Broad Somerford. He opened his eyes wide when he learnt that I had walked in to Malmesbury and wider still when I told him that I was going to walk back again.

I left Malmesbury at 5 o'clock and reached home at 7.30.

Thursday 11 March 1875

It was a fine clear starry night, and the young moon was shining brightly. Near the school I overtook a lad of eighteen walking slowly and wearily, who asked me how far it was to Sutton. He said he had walked down to-day from Broad Hinton, 7 miles the other side of Swindon. He was seeking work and could find none. He was very tired and out of spirits. He had just asked the Sutton baker to give him a lift in his trap, promising to give him a pint of beer, but the baker surlily bade him to keep his beer to himself and refused to pull up and take the lad in, giving him leave, however, to hang on behind the trap from Broad Somerford to Seagry. He had tried to get a bed at Somerford, but the inn was full of navvies who are making the new railroad to Malmesbury from Dauntsey.

There was no room for him in the inn. I thought it might encourage and cheer the lad up if I kept company along the road to Sutton, so we walked together and I showed him the short cut across the fields. As we went we fell into talk and the lad began to be confidential and to tell me something of his story. It was a simple, touching tale.

'I was born,' said the lad, 'at a little village near here called Corston, but I have been knocking about the country looking for work. I have some aunts in Corston.'

'But have you no father or mother?' I asked. The simple chance question touched a heart still tender and bruised with a great sorrow, and opened the floodgates of his soul. The lad suddenly burst into tears.

'My mother was buried to-day,' he sobbed. 'I walked up to Broad Hinton yesterday, to try to get work, for my stepfather would not keep me any longer and I could get no work in Corston. I would have stayed to follow my mother to the grave but I had no black clothes except a jacket, and couldn't get any. She was the best friend I had in the world, and the only one. I was with her when she died. She said I had better die too, along with her, for I should only be knocked about in a hard world and there would be no one to care for me. And I've found her words true and thought upon them often enough already,' added the poor boy bitterly, with another burst of heart-broken tears.

'My name is Henry Estcourt Ferris,' the lad went on, in answer to some questions of mine. 'My father's name is Estcourt. He is a labouring man working in Wales as a boiler maker. He ran away from my Mother and forsook her six months before I was born. My Mother's maiden name,' said the poor boy with some hesitation, 'was Ellen Ferris.'

Alas, the old, old story. Trust misplaced, promises broken, temptation, sin and sorrow, and the sins of the parents visited upon the children. It was pleasant and touching to hear the grateful way in which the lad spoke of the kindness of the Pollen family to him when he was a child. 'Miss Jessie', 'Miss Constant', 'Miss Katie' were familiar household names to him, and he named them tenderly with a sacred gentle reverence, lingering upon the old sweet memories with a sad regretful affection.

When we got to Sutton we went to three places, two inns and a private lodging house, to try to get the lad a bed. A villager in the street told us of the lodging house, but everywhere the lad was refused a bed, and from each house in succession he turned wearily and hopelessly away with a faint protest and remonstrance and a lingering request that the good people would please to try if they could not put him up, but in vain, and we plodded on again towards Chippenham where he knew he could get a bed at the Little George. The poor fellow was very humble and grateful. 'I shouldn't have been near so far along the road as this, if it hadn't been for you, Sir,' he said gratefully. 'You've kind of livened and 'ticed me along.'

I cheered him up as well as I could and gave him a bit of good advice. He hoped to get a place at Chippenham Great Market to-morrow. The lights of Langley Fitzurse shone brightly through the dark night. ''Tis a long road,' said the lad wearily. At the Hillocks stile we parted at length with a clasp of the hand and a kindly 'Goodbye' and I saw the last, for ever, probably, in this world, of the motherless boy.

It is hard not to be moved by this piece. Whatever happened to Henry Estcourt Ferris? If he was eighteen then he might have lived into the 1940s or '50s, but something in the story suggests that he would not make old bones.

The same, unhappily, applied to Kilvert. Only four years later, and with his marriage only five weeks old, he died of peritonitis. He did not live to see forty, but his 39 years were lived with love, and his warm vitality survives through his diaries.

Another diarist, similarly named but in no way as talented, was John Simpson Calvertt, who was born in 1829, farmed at Leafield, near Witney, and kept a diary from 1875 until his death in 1900. His entries are brief and deal primarily with farming matters, interspersed with doleful comments on the weather. His major interests apart from farming were the royal family and national events. But perhaps his most amusing entries are those for 31 December of each year:

Yanworth

The Trout Inn, Lechlade

31 December 1879

Wind and rain most of the day – no work done!!! So ends the most *ruinously* ugly *seasoned* year, of *this century*.

31 December 1880

Foggy night – with rain at 7 a.m. till night, then Fog!!! Been wet, with very little sunshine, since 20th April last!!!

The past year has been famous for *Terror, Murders* and lawlessness in Ireland – The Closure in Parliament – The Egyptian Army Revolt – Cetewayo's return to Zululand – &c.

Been one of the *most hindering* years for Farming I ever experienced – from *20th April last* . . .

An August entry raises a slightly more hopeful note. The rain stopped the harvest work, but Calvertt had at least some consolation:

27 August 1885

Rainy morning – stopped all harvest work.
Cricket: Gloucestershire v. Middlesex

	348	110 1st innings
		233 2nd do.

Mr. W.G. Grace played magnificently *thro'* the Game, and carried his bat for 221, and afterwards bowled 10 of his opponents' wickets out of 15!!!

31 December 1885

. . . The past year has been the most *unprofitable* for Farming I have experienced since I began in 1852!!!

31 December 1887

Much of the past year, been the *worst* on *record* for *Farmers* – the weather set in, sunny & hot from 10th June

for *3 months*, consequently no after-maths – half a crop of Spring Corn – Grass burnt up – a fifth of a Turnip Crop, and the young Clovers, more than half scorched up – *three-fourths* of the Wheats, good crops, at 28s. to 31s. – for Reds – Barley 23s. – Oats 15s. – Ruination to *Landlords, & Tenants*!!!

31 December 1888

The hardest frost during this Autumn, and Winter: but could plough.

One of the worst years on record for Agriculture – cold, late Spring – wet Haytime for 6 or 8 weeks – late, bad-yielding, Corn Harvest – but average crops roots – good plant young Clovers, and grass much of it, eatable till Xmas. . .

Not all of it was rain and ruin for John Calvertt, however. He succeeded in making a good living, for all his complaints, and enjoyed the life of a gentleman farmer with well over 1,000 acres of Cotswold land to his name:

25 January 1890

Met Hounds at Sturdy's Castle . . . at 2 p.m. I left them, in wind & rain, trying Sq. Hall's Covers at Barton!!!

Yesterday had the best run of the Season from Eyford – 15 miles in 1 hour & 30 min!!!

Cherington

Hailey

On the same day that Calvertt was retreating home out of the wind and rain this letter was printed in the GLOUCESTERSHIRE CHRONICLE:

25 January 1890

In looking over an old scrapbook today, I came upon the following copy of a paper sent to the Crier of the city of Gloucester 'to make proclamation of the annual sports of Whitsuntide, 1836':

'Cooper's Hill Weke to commence on Wits Monday *per sisly* at 3 o'clock. 2 cheeses to be ron for. 1 Plain Cake to be *green* for. 1 do. do. to be jumpt in the bag for. *Horings* to be Dipt in the toob for. Set of ribons to be dansed for. *Shimey* to be ron for. Belt to be rosled for. A bladder of snuff to be *chatred* for by *hold wimming*.'

This is hard to translate 'per sisly'. The 'green' was the old country pursuit of grinning or gurning – pulling funny faces through a horsecollar. Contestants were not allowed to use their hands to pull their face around, and it usually helped your chances of winning if you did not have a tooth in your head.

'Shimey' is a chemise, and 'hold wimming' is presumably 'old women'. The letter created some interest, and another correspondent recalled the cheese-rolling of his youth.

8 February 1890

I was amused when I read in your columns a fortnight ago the copy of the bill announcing Cooper's Hill wake. The master of the ceremonies usually employed the Gloucester town crier to 'bawl' the proclamation through the streets. The orthography of these original announcements is invaluable, because it affords a kind of phonograph of the old Gloucestershire or Cotswold dialect.

Some of my earliest recollections are associated with Cooper's Hill wake, which, in old days, was a festivity of some magnitude. Old John Jones, of Cooper's Hill, and

the late Sir William Hicks, of Witcomb Park, were great patrons of the annual saturnalia.

I can recollect Organ, the master of ceremonies, who was a fine, tall, handsome fellow. He used to appear upon the summit of the hill, dressed in a white linen chemise, adorned with ribbons of all the colours of the rainbow. His hat was also decked with ribbons, and around his waist he wore the belt for which the wrestlers were to struggle, the winner claiming honour as champion wrestler for the year.

Organ's advent was hailed with shouts by the hilarious multitude; and no Caesar attired in Imperial robe of Tyrian dye could have been more proud than he was of his milk-white 'smock', for the old English name and the Frenchified 'chemise' was that by which the garment was known to all.

'Old Gipsey Jack' was always there, with his Asiatic face and his old black fiddle; his wife with eyes like the eagles, a face as brown as a 'bannut' bud and hair as black as a thunder cloud, was there also, with her dingy tambourine; and to the tum-tum of the fiddle and the jingle of the tambourine the country lads and lasses danced to their hearts' content. Organ was the judge of merit in these exercises, and I think the most graceful dancer generally won most of the ribbons. It was a pretty spectacle, and I never witnessed any impropriety. The peasantry were not so learned or so 'refined' as they are now supposed to be; but they were contented and happy when:

> At the wake of Cooper's Hill
> Each Jack appeared with charming Jill.

In days of yore, not only the daughters of the peasants, but those also of the farmers, mingled in the throng of merry dancers, and how proud were 'Jane' and 'Mary' of the ribbons they had won by their agility and endurance! The wrestling was not a pleasant spectacle, despite its ardent admirers and votaries. A man of pugilistic build and character formed a human circle by beating the turf, and alternately the toes of the crowd, with a long ground-ash stick, and shouted 'A ring! A ring!' When the arena was formed, the struggle commenced.

I have seen a couple of stalwart fellows, with sinew and tendon of iron, struggle fiercely, not to say ferociously, for the mastery. What a shout of exultation went up when the victor landed his opponent fairly on his back on the sward! It was surprising how human limbs could be so strained and kicked without the thews cracking and the bones breaking. These brutal trials of strength may have made the race hardy, tough, and valiant. To me, however, the spectacle was brutal and inhuman.

I once met an aged athlete who had been the champion at Cooper's Hill, but had become a cripple. 'John,' I asked, 'what is the matter?'

'Why, Mayster Harry, I ha' got a nashun bod leg.'

'How is that, John?'

'Mayster Harry, the follies o' my youth. If I had my days to go over agen, I'd never stond up to ha' my legs kicked to pieces at Cooper's Hill wake. I ha' larned this, thot our blessed Meeker nivver made our precious limbs to be kicked at vor other volks' amusement.'

The grinning through 'hoses collards' was a grand amusement. Some of the faces distorted to produce the 'best grin' would have puzzled Lavater and delighted Hogarth. Dipping in a tub of water for oranges and apples, and bobbing for penny loaves smeared with hot treacle need no description.

The grand climax to the annual revel was running down the frightful declivity of the hill after a cheese. It was a perilous feat; but young fellows were ever willing to risk the danger. An old man described the cheese as being 'Hard as Fayrur's heart, or the nether millstone.'

I have seen the cheese bound down the hill and over a stone wall into the ground beyond. I have seen it in the hands of the winner without the symptom of a crack in it or the sign of an abrasion. To have run down the terrible descent was perilous; to have eaten the trophy must have been a more dangerous feat than its capture.

Racing for the prize chemise was to me the most degrading part of the revels; but there were plenty of girls for the contest, until a sad catastrophy occurred. On one occasion a young woman outpaced her competitors, reached the goal first – and there dropped dead!

After the wake was over, ruffianism commenced. The village feuds, grudges, and personal quarrels were then settled. Hats were thrown into the air, rings were formed, and sanguinary and prolonged fights followed. It should be mentioned to the credit of the 'fair sex' that they usually left the hill before these displays began; but sometimes a poor girl lingered to implore her sweetheart not to fight.

Meanwhile, John Calvertt was still having problems with his farming:

31 December 1891

The past [*year*] has been the most wretched, ruinous year's weather, for farming, I ever experienced since 1852!!!

Jas. Francis Mason, sent me 2 brace Ck. Pheasants!!!

31 December 1892

So ends in a keen frosty 8 days Rime the wretched year 1892: for Agriculturists: for 'Produce Prices', the lowest on Record!!!

1891 & 1892, have proved the most ruinous of my life?

In 1893 an exceptionally dry spell caused the following entry in Dearman Birchall's diary.

Stretton-on-Fosse

Sherston

13 April 1893

This is an extraordinary season. We have not had a drop of rain for about six weeks and almost constant sunshine with coldish nights, frost even up to 10 degrees, but the wonderful dryness in the air has prevented the blossom suffering. The country is in a blaze from the pears, plums and even apples. The horse chestnut on the drive close to the house is in full flower . . .

Surprisingly, Calvertt does not complain about the dry weather, but it does warrant repeated comment:

18 April 1893

Heard Cuckoo – 1st. time. Cherry trees in full bloom – very early.

30 April 1893

Nine weeks today since rain fell to any amount – a Drought prevails mostly over the whole of Europe. . .

7 May 1893

Brilliant sunny morning, with cold East Wind – not had a rainy morning for *10 weeks*!!!
Strawberries, Hawthorn, Laburnams, Azaleas, been in full Bloom for days.
Prince George, the Duke of York: to marry Princess Mary of Teck: to the satisfaction of *all*!!!

31 December 1893

Trees look very pretty, laden with frozen Fog, with brilliant sunshine.
Of *all wretched* years, in Agriculture, this takes the *Cake*!!!

But what is this? A sign of mellowing?

31 December 1898

1898 has been a very *productive*, fine weather year; *all over* England!!

Away from gentlemen farmers, 1897 brought the publication of one of the most memorable of Cotswold books, A COTSWOLD VILLAGE, *by Joseph Arthur Gibbs. The book went through three editions in as many years, the third, in 1899, coming out shortly after the author's death at the age of just thirty-one.*
Gibbs came from a wealthy family, but he had that ease of manner that made him at home with all kinds of people. A villager in Ablington, on hearing of his death, wrote: 'He went in and out as a friend among them', and his observations on village life around Bibury are touchingly evocative:

Every village seems to possess its share of quaint, curious people, but I cannot help thinking that our little hamlet has a more varied assortment of oddities than is usually to be met with in so small a place.
First of all there is the man who nobody ever sees. Although he has lived in robust health for the past twenty years in the very centre of the hamlet, his face is unknown to half the inhabitants. Twice only has the writer set eyes on him. When a political contest is proceeding he becomes comparatively bold; at such times he has even been met with in the bar of the village 'public', where he has been known to sit discussing the chances of the candidate like any ordinary being. But an election is absolutely necessary if this strange individual is to be drawn out of his hiding-place.
The only other occasion on which we have set eyes on him was on a lovely summer's evening, just after sunset: we observed him peeping at us over a hedge, for all the world like the 'Spectator' when he was staying with Sir Roger de Coverley. He is supposed to come out at sunset,

like the foxes and the bats, and has been seen in the distance on bright moonlight nights striding over the Cotswold uplands. If anyone approach him, he hurries away in the opposite direction; yet he is not queer in the head, but strong and in the prime of life.

Then there is that very common character 'the village imposter'. After having been turned away by half a dozen different farmers, because he never did a stroke of work, he manages to get on the sick list at the 'great house'. Long after his ailment has been cured he will be seen daily going up to the manor house for his allowance of meat; somehow or other he 'can't get a job nohow'. The fact is, he has got the name of being an idle scoundrel, and no farmer will take him on. It is some time before you are able to find him out; for as he goes decidedly lame as he passes you in the village street, he generally manages to persuade you that he is very ill. Like a fool, you take compassion on him, and give him an ounce of 'baccy' and half a crown. For some months he hangs about where he thinks you will be passing, craving a pipe of tobacco; until one day, when you are having a talk with some other honest toiler, he will give you a hint that you are being imposed on.

When a loafer of this sort finds that he can get nothing more out of you, he moves his family and goods to some other part of the country; he then begins the old game with somebody else, borrowing a sovereign off you for the expense of moving. As for gratitude, he never thinks of it. The other day a man with a 'game leg' who was, in spite of his lameness, a good example of 'the village imposter', in taking his departure from our hamlet, gave out 'that there was no thanks due to the big 'ouse for the benefits he had received, for it was writ in the *manor parchments* as how he was to have meat three times a week and blankets at Christmas as long as he was out of work'.

It is so difficult to discriminate between the good and the bad amongst the poor, and it is impossible not to feel pity for a man who has nothing but the workhouse to look forward to, even if he has come down in the world through his own folly. To those who are living in luxury the conditions under which the poorer classes earn their daily bread, and the wretched prospect which old age or ill health presents to them, must ever offer scope for deep reflection and compassion.

We have many other interesting characters in our village; human nature varies so delightfully that just as with faces so each individual character has something to distinguish it from the rest of the world. The old-fashioned autocratic farmer of the old school is there of course, and a rare good specimen he is of a race that has almost disappeared. Then we have the village lunatic, whose mania is 'religious enthusiasm'. If you go to call on him, he will ask you 'if you are saved', and explain to you how his own salvation was brought about. Unfortunately one of his hobbies is to keep fowls and pigs in his house so that fleas are more or less numerous there, and your visits are consequently few and far between.

The village 'quack', who professes to cure every complaint under the sun, either in mankind, horses, dogs, or anything else by means of herbs, buttonholes you sometimes in the village street. If once he starts talking, you know that you are 'booked' for the day. He is rather a 'bore', and is uncommonly fond of quoting the Scriptures in support of his theories. But there is something about the man one cannot help liking. His wonderful infallibility in curing disease is set down by himself to divine inspiration. Many a vision has he seen. Unfortunately his doctrines, though excellent in theory, are seldom successful in practice. An excellent prescription which I am informed completely cured a man of indigestion is one of his mixtures 'last thing at night' and the first chapter of St. John carefully perused and digested on top.

I called on the old gentleman the other day, and persuaded him to give me a short lecture. The following is the gist of what he said: 'First of all you must know that

Cirencester Mop

the elder is good for anything in the world, but especially good for swellings. If you put some of the leaves on your face, they will cure toothache in five minutes. Then for the nerves there's nothing like the berries of ivy. Yarrow makes a splendid ointment; and be sure and remember Solomon's seal for bruises, and comfrey for 'hurts' and broken bones.

'Camomile cures indigestion, and ash-tree buds make a stout man thin. Soak some ash leaves in hot water, and you will have a drink that is better than any tea, and destroys the 'gravel'. Walnut-tree bark is a splendid emetic; and mountain flax, which grows everywhere on the Cotswolds, is uncommon good for the "innards". 'Ettles [*nettles*] is good for stings. Damp them and rub them on to a "wapse" sting, and they will take away the pain directly.'

On my suggesting that stinging nettles were rather a desperate remedy, he assured me that they acted as a blister, and counteracted the 'wapse'.

'Now, I'll tell you an uncommon good thing to preserve the teeth,' he went on, 'and that is to *brush* them once or twice a week. You buys a brush at the chymists, you know; they makes them specially for it. Oh, 'tis a capital good thing to cleanse the teeth occasionally!'

A strange looking traveller, with slouching gait and mouldy wideawake hat, passes through the hamlet occasionally, leading a donkey in a cart. This is one of the old-fashioned hawkers. These men are usually poachers, or the receivers of poached goods. They are not averse to paying a small sum for a basket of trout or a few partridges, pheasants, hares or rabbits in the game season, whilst in spring they deal in a small way in the eggs of game birds.

As often as not this class of man is accompanied by a couple of dogs, marvellously trained in the art of hunting the coverts and 'retrieving' a pheasant or a rabbit which may be crouching in the underwood . . . One never finds out much about these gentry from the natives. Even the keeper is reticent on the subject. 'A sart of a harf-witted fellow,' is Tom Peregrine's description of this very suspicious looking traveller.

The better sort of carrier, who calls daily at the great house with all sorts of goods and parcels from the big town seven miles off, is occasionally not averse to a little poaching in the roadside fields among the hares. The carriers are a great feature of these rural villages; they are generally good fellows, though some of them are a bit too fond of the bottle on Saturday nights.

Gibbs also observed the bottle being hit during the Cirencester mop fair, and being the good Victorian gentleman he was, he was not impressed. When he surmised that the event would soon die out, however, he was indulging in wishful thinking. The fair still visits the town to this day.

One of the old institutions which still remain in the Cotswolds is the annual 'mop', or hiring fair. At Cirencester these take place twice in October. Every labouring man in the district hurries into the town, where all sorts of entertainments are held in the market-place, including 'whirly-go-rounds', discordant music and the usual 'shows' which go to make up a country fair.

'Hiring' used to be the great feature of these fairs. In the days before local newspapers were invented every sort of servant, from a farm bailiff to a maid-of-all-work, was hired for the year at the annual mop. The word 'mop' is derived from an old custom which ordained that the maid-servants who came to find situations should bring their badge of office with them to the fair. They came with their brooms and mops, just as a carter would tie a piece of whipcord to his coat, and a shepherd's hat would be decorated with a tuft of wool . . .

Now that these old fairs no longer answer the purpose for which they existed for hundreds of years, they will doubtless gradually die out. And they have their drawbacks. An occasion of this kind is always associated with a good deal of drunkenness; the old market-place of Cirencester for a few days in each autumn becomes a regular pandemonium. It is marvellous how quickly all traces of the great show are swept away and the place once more settles down to the normal condition of an old-fashioned though well-to-do country town.

Times, indeed, were changing and Gibbs, in the late 1890s in Bibury, realised that a revolution in personal transport would make yet more impact on country life. His credentials as a prophet, however, are somewhat undermined by the fact that he saw the threat coming not from the car – but the pushbike!

It was at about this time that the artist and craftsman William Morris, with his 'old house by the Thames' at Kelmscott, was declaring Bibury 'the most beautiful village in England'. It is still an idyllic spot in its location, beside the river beneath densely wooded hills, and no more so than when the visitors have gone home and the only sounds are the babble of the water and the roosting birds in the hillside rookery. But for most who pass through it today, with cars such a dominant feature beside the stream, it must fall some way short of Morris's big build-up. If only the world could have contented itself with Gibbs's bicycles!

It is probable that the bicycle will cause a larger demand for remote country houses. To the writer, who previously to this summer had never experienced the poetry of motion which the bicycle coasting downhill, with a smooth road and a favourable wind, undoubtedly constitutes, the invention seems of the greatest utility. It brings places sixty miles apart within our immediate neighbourhood.

Let the south wind blow and we can be in quaint old Tewkesbury, thirty miles away, in less than three hours. A northerly gale will land us at the 'Blowing-stone' and the old White Horse of Berkshire with less labour than it takes to walk a mile. Yet in the old days these twenty miles were a great gulf fixed between the Gloucestershire natives and the 'chaw-bacons' over the boundary.

Their very language is as different as possible. To this day the villagers who went to the last 'scouring of the horse' and saw the old-fashioned backsword play talk of the expedition with as much pride as if they had made a pilgrimage to the Antipodes.

The lifestyle Gibbs discovered in Bibury was destroyed by the First World War, and any attempt to return to it was confounded by the advent of electricity and the motor car.

Another pre-war visitor and commentator was Ernest Temple Thurston, author of THE FLOWER OF GLOSTER. He was a prolific and popular novelist early this century, and this book was something of a digression from his normal style.

The FLOWER was a narrow-boat, and his meandering journeys around the canals of Middle England took him along the Thames & Severn only a matter of months before it was closed to traffic in 1911. The pride of the canal then, of course – and it will be again if a small band of restoration enthusiasts ever get their way – was the Sapperton Tunnel, at 3,817 yards the longest in Britain when it was opened in 1789.

As a recorder of precise historical fact Temple Thurston was not always the most reliable witness, as we discovered earlier with his account of the king at Sapperton. But his first-hand reporting was of the best, and it is pleasing to have such a detailed description of the old chore of 'legging', in which the canal craft were propelled through the tunnel by men pushing their feet against the roof and walls:

The passage through the tunnel of Sapperton, which, on a sudden bend of the canal, opens a deep black mouth into the heart of the hills, was the only time when the voyage of the *Flower of Gloster* had in it the sense of stirring adventure. Into the grim darkness you glide and, within half an hour, are lost in a lightless cavern where the drip

drip of the clammy water sounds incessantly in your ears.

Some time ago, when there was more constant traffic on this canal, there were professional leggers to carry you through; for there is no tow-path, and the barge must be propelled by the feet upon the side walls of the tunnel. Now that the barges pass so seldom, this profession has become obsolete. There are no leggers now.

For four hours Eynsham Harry and I lay upon our sides on the wings that are fitted to the boat for that purpose, and legged every inch of the two and three-quarter miles. It is no gentle job. Countless were the number of times I looked on ahead to that faint pin-point of light; but by such infinite degrees did it grow larger as we neared the end, that I thought we should never reach it.

'What used the leggers to be paid?' I asked after the first mile, when it seemed all sensation had gone out of my limbs and they were working merely in obedience to the despairing effort of my will.

'Five shillings, sir, for a loaded boat. Two and six for an empty one.'

I groaned.

'A pound wouldn't satisfy me,' I said.

'No, sur, I suspects not. It's always easier to do these things for nothing.'

For an hour that was all we said. For an hour I legged away, thinking how true that casual statement was – 'It's always easier to do these things for nothing.' It is – always. All labour would be play were it not for payment . . .

But one does not think of this sort of thing for long while legging it through Sapperton Tunnel. A drip of shiny water on one's face is quite enough to upset the most engrossing contemplation. I saw the pin-point of light growing to the pin's head, and still we laboured on, only resting a few moments to light a fresh piece of candle or take breath.

It was evening when we came out into the light again and, though the sun had set, with shadows falling every-where, it almost dazzled me. A barge in the next lock rose above the lock's arms, with every line cut out against the pale sky.

Towards the end of the journey, with thoughts of busy London looming, Temple Thurston decides he would like one last lunch of country eggs. It involves a two-mile walk from the barge to Marston Meysey, but after a brief encounter with a suspicious guard dog he finds that the young girl in the shop makes his walk well worth the effort:

'He doesn't like strangers,' said the little girl.

'Whereas you trust everybody,' said I.

'It depends what they look like,' she replied.

It was as good as asking me to speak of myself, and as no man refuses such invitation when it is proffered him, I asked her if she meant that she passed me as trustworthy. She eyed me shyly, making me remember that I had not been in the company of her sex for one whole month.

'Well?' said I – and as I said it, I felt my eye meet hers. Now whether there was that in my expression which conveyed my thoughts to her intuition, I would not swear, but she blushed. Then she looked charming, and her eyes dropped . . .

'Now hadn't I better tell you what I want?'

She nodded her head and, because she thought we were about to begin business, raised her eyes again. Accordingly I talked business steadily – the business about the eggs – for five minutes. The woman who has said she will never speak to you again is always amenable to conversation if you talk business. You may mean what you like – in fact, the more you mean, the more ready is she to talk. Whenever I stopped and she found me watching her, she would say no more. So I asked that the eggs might be boiled then and there.

'I want them for lunch,' said I, 'and have got no place to boil them in.'

Snowshill

'I thought you said you were on a barge,' she replied. 'Haven't you got a stove in the cabin?'

'Thief!' said the dog in the barrel.

'That's quite true,' I answered, and I took no notice of the dog. 'We have a stove and a saucepan and an egg-timer. I told the lie in order to stop a little longer and talk to you . . .'

The little girl took the four brown eggs without a word, put them in a saucepan with some water and placed them on a fire which was already burning in a little niche in the wall. She just added a stick or two, pouring a few drops of paraffin over it to make the whole blaze up.

'I want them hard,' said I.

'You shall have them hard,' said she.

For a while then, we stood together and watched the water boil. Once I looked out of the corner of my eyes to her face to find her staring down into the saucepan, her whole expression full of contemplation.

'A penny,' said I suddenly.

She started.

'One penny,' I repeated.

'Not for twenty pence,' said she.

'Which means,' said I, with that intuitive egotism of my sex, 'that you're thinking about me.'

'Do you think a thought about you would be worth twenty pence?' she asked.

'Thief!' said the dog in the barrel.

'Not to speak,' said I, and I ignored the dog again. 'It 'ud be worth more than twenty pence to conceal.'

She bent down and looked into the saucepan.

'It's boiling,' said she.

'So am I,' said I, 'with curiosity.'

'How are you going to take the eggs?' she asked – 'In your pocket?'

'I'll take them,' said I, 'as you give them to me, in my hand.'

'Then I'll put them in a bag,' said she.

And so she did when they were boiled. With her little hand wrinkled already with hard work, she held out the bag by one corner and I took it by the other.

'And now,' said I, 'how much?' But somehow I hated asking it.

'Two pence,' she replied. I don't think she minded in the least. It is only men who are sentimentalists over these matters. They have no head for business when they have a heart to count the coin.

'But two pence!' I exclaimed. 'There were four – four eggs.'

'Halfpenny each,' she replied.

'But the boiling?'

'I won't charge you for that,' she said.

'You can charge me anything you like for the boiling,' said I, stooping to bribery, as is the habit of the best of us – 'you can charge me anything you like if you'll tell me what you were thinking about just now.'

'I won't charge you for the boiling,' said she.

'Fool!' said the dog in the barrel.

This last incident tells us a few things. It perhaps symbolises how the Cotswolds, those closest to London in particular, were becoming increasingly frequented by rather smart and clever visitors. It gives us some insight into the Edwardian version of the age-old pursuit of chatting up innocent country girls. And it perhaps also hints at the personal turmoil of Temple Thurston, who was in his early thirties when he had this encounter with a child probably less than half his age in Marston Meysey. He was married three times and divorced by two of his wives, the first time in 1910. The FLOWER OF GLOSTER voyage was doubtless an attempt to escape from that trauma.

Though there is something archaic about Temple Thurston's writing, he made his waterway voyage only a decade or so before the schooldays described in that most celebrated Cotswold reminiscence, Laurie Lee's CIDER WITH ROSIE.

Of course Mr Lee's book did not come out until 1959, and it was written not only with the benefit of hindsight but with consummate artistic skill. One of its key elements is the imminence of change – change for young Loll and for the village of Slad – and the author transports us from a community little changed in centuries to one fast learning to dance to the rhythm of modern life.

Laurie Lee was three when his family first arrived in Slad, and this was the timeless world in which he found himself:

The village to which our family had come was a scattering of some twenty to thirty houses down the south-east slope of a valley. The valley was narrow, steep, and almost entirely cut off; it was also a funnel for winds, a channel for the floods and a jungly, bird-crammed, insect-hopping sun-trap whenever there happened to be any sun. It was not high and open like the Windrush country, but had secret origins, having been gouged from the Escarpment by the melting ice-caps some time before we got there. The old flood-terraces still showed on the slopes, along which the cows walked sideways. Like an island, it was possessed of curious survivals – rare orchids and Roman snails; and there were chemical qualities in the limestone-springs which gave the women pre-Raphaelite goitres. The sides of the valley were rich in pasture and the crests heavily covered in beechwoods.

Living down there was like living in a bean-pod; one could see nothing but the bed one lay in. Our horizon of woods was the limit of our world. For weeks on end the trees moved in the wind with a dry roaring which seemed a natural utterance of the landscape. In winter they ringed us with frozen spikes, and in summer they oozed over the lips of the hills like layers of thick green lava. Mornings, they steamed with mist or sunshine, and almost every evening threw streamers above us, reflecting sunsets we were too hidden to see.

Water was the most active thing in the valley, arriving in the long rains from Wales. It would drip all day from clouds and trees, from roofs and eaves and noses. It broke open roads, carved its way through gardens, and filled the ditches with sucking noises. Men and horses walked about in wet sacking, birds shook rainbows from sodden branches, and streams ran from holes, and back into holes, like noisy underground trains.

I remember, too, the light on the slopes, long shadows in tufts and hollows, with cattle, brilliant as painted china, treading their echoing shapes. Bees blew like cake-crumbs through the golden air, white butterflies like sugared wafers, and when it wasn't raining a diamond dust took over, which veiled and yet magnified all things.

Most of the cottages were built of Cotswold stone and were roofed by split-stone tiles. The tiles grew a kind of golden moss which sparkled like crystallized honey. Behind the cottages were long steep gardens full of cabbages, fruit-bushes, roses, rabbit-hutches, earth-closets, bicycles, and pigeon-lofts. In the very sump of the valley wallowed the Squire's Big House – once a fine, though modest sixteenth-century manor, to which a Georgian facade had been added.

The villagers themselves had three ways of living: working for the Squire, or on the farms, or down in the cloth-mills at Stroud. Apart from the Manor, and the ample cottage gardens – which were an insurance against hard times – all other needs were supplied by a church, a chapel, a vicarage, a manse, a wooden hut, a pub – and the village school.

There is little in that account of Slad in around 1920 that would not have applied a century earlier – and in spirit, if not in detail, a hundred years before that, and before that. But what a different story some fifteen or so years on, when it was Laurie Lee's turn to discover what lay beyond those encircling woods:

The girls were to marry; the Squire was dead; buses ran and the towns were nearer. We began to shrug off the valley and look more to the world, where pleasures were more anonymous and tasty. They were coming fast, and we were nearly ready for them. Each week Miss Bagnall held her penny dances where girls' shapes grew more familiar. For a penny one could swing them through Lancers and Two-Steps across the resinous floor of the Hut – but if one swung them entirely off their feet then Miss B locked the piano and went home . . .

Time squared itself, and the village shrank, and distances crept nearer. The sun and moon, which once rose from our hill, rose from London now in the east. One's body was no longer a punching ball, to be thrown against trees and banks, but a telescoping totem crying strange demands few of which we could yet supply. In the faces of the villagers one could see one's change, and in their habits their own change also. The horses had died; few people kept pigs any more, but spent their spare time buried in engines. The flutes and cornets, the gramophones with horns, the wind harps were thrown away – now wireless aerials searched the electric sky for the music of the Savoy Orpheans. Old men in the pubs sang 'As I Walked Out', then walked out and never came back.

In the middle 1930s, at the time Laurie Lee was turning his back on Slad, C. Henry Warren was settling into life in the Cotswolds after an army and teaching career that had taken him from the Middle East to the Home Counties. After four years in Gloucestershire he published A COTSWOLD YEAR in 1936, a month-by-month account chronicling the changing seasons and commenting on local life and lore.

The book begins with December, possibly because there was a good Christmas tale to tell:

December 24.

When we got to Miserden, the village was shut in an intense darkness: no pointed junipers thrust their shadowy outlines against the sky and only an occasional lamp in somebody's cottage window declared that not everybody was asleep. Most of the men folk of the village must have been in the Carpenter's Arms, so large an assembly filled the smoke-dense room when we opened the door. There must have been thirty men present, sitting and standing about, talking and laughing, while the landlord hurried in and out among them, throwing a joke over his shoulders as he attended to the orders fired at him from all quarters.

A wood-fire filled the large open fire-place, over which there were arranged a row of bright brass candle-sticks and some shining steel spits. No game of darts monopolised the space and the conversation; no unsightly beer or tobacco advertisements spoiled the clean, washed walls; and instead of the usual smoky and inadequate oil-lamp a smart petrol-lamp threw abundance of light everywhere. I do not know a more attractive inn anywhere in the Cotswolds, and certainly I have never seen one so full of jovial good-will as the Carpenter's Arms was this evening.

Here were men who preferred sociable talk to silent drinks and games in a corner: even the inevitable 'oldest inhabitant', a man of eighty-six, mingled with the rest, his hand cupping his ear to catch the latest piece of local scandal and his eyes lighting up with pleasure as he bandied racy quips with his friends. Song after song filled the smoke-blue room, everybody joining in with gusto, and quite drowning the impromptu accompaniment of the fiddler, who wandered in and out among the singing crowd, shutting his eyes and sweeping his bow up to the ceiling.

Now and then, one of the men would sing a solo, while the fiddler stood at his side and the rest of the company joined heartily in the chorus. One of the best songs tonight was a masterly performance of 'The Barley Mow', and how good it was to hear this grand old folk-song removed from the artificial atmosphere of the drawing-room or

River Bank near Southrop

Winchcombe

festival, and sung by men who have lived the sentiments they were singing!

But perhaps my fancy was most seized by a ballad I had never heard before. It was sung by a middle-aged man whose absence of any tonal sense was more than compensated for by a rare vigour and naturalness. His ballad was all about a man who sailed abroad, taking with him a wonderful bird in a gilded cage. When he had settled down in his new country (obviously one of our colonies) the men used to gather around him to listen to the singing of that bird, their hearts almost ceasing to beat at hearing once again a thrush from their own far-away homeland . . . Too soon the landlord called 'Time, gentlemen!' For a while, we stood outside the door, in the pitch-black night, tidying up the tag-ends of conversation, then made for home. 'Goodnight, Bill! Goodnight, Jack! And a happy Christmas!'

By and large that was the traditional side of the country scene that Warren was happy to record, and it doubtless fell in well with what he wanted and expected from his retirement in the Cotswolds. Down the valley in Slad Laurie Lee, in the springtime of his adult life, could see only change. The retiree Warren much preferred to stress the other side of the coin, though he glimpsed village life of another sort when he visited Whiteway, the colony founded in the early years of this century by followers of Tolstoy's principles of self-sufficiency and freedom from outside bureaucracy.

Close to Miserden, Whiteway today has come a long way from those original ideals, but it is still a place for rugged individualists who can turn their hands to practical and artistic tasks, and in appearance it remains the most atypical of Cotswold villages. This is how Warren found it in the middle 1930s:

As I came out of those quiet upland lanes, where the hedges were still bright with the red of autumn, and found myself suddenly overlooking the colony, it was almost as if the countryside had been violated. Dozens of bungalows, of all shapes and sizes and colours, were scattered about, more like my idea of the Medicine Hat of fifty years ago than of a brave new world of the twentieth century . . . When you build yourself a house, surely some thought ought to be given to the fact that other people besides yourself will have to look at it? But evidently these colonists did not think so. Perhaps they held that it does not matter what the outside is like so long as all is fair within. And perhaps they were right.

Anyway, there stood the tin-roofed huts and the oddly assorted bungalows. The roads were fair: considering that they were home-made affairs they might well have been much worse. Gay late flowers grew trustfully along their sides, as if they had no need to fear acquisitive fingers. It seemed a happy augury. Everywhere I came upon notice-boards announcing teas and refreshments and homecrafts. I had been told that once upon a time the place had quite a reputation locally for its concerts. But apparently all that is changed now: chamber-music has given place to the radio. And I certainly saw no signs of that happy activity which was an integral part in the original conception of the colony.

During the course of the afternoon I had a talk with one of the oldest 'settlers'. Her calm and her courtesy, her dignity and quietness, her genuine culture, did much to dispel my rather disheartening first impressions of the place. Perhaps, I thought, I had let the shell of things influence me too much after all. My informant admitted that much water had flowed under the bridges, so to speak, since that far-away gesture of burning the title deeds. From the original five the number of inhabitants had grown to eighty. All the land had been parcelled out and there was now no room for newcomers. I gathered that the early colonists, though received in a friendly enough manner by the neighbourhood, had met with some opposition from the authorities. There was the incident of a distrained piano, the only one in the place; and there was the no less serious (though more amusing) incident of the distrained steamroller, a present from some wealthy well-wisher.

I asked what had been the credentials necessary for admittance into the colony in those days. 'None in particular,' I was told. 'Someone came along, seemed interested and deserving, and their application was considered by the joint assembly. If they seemed likely aspirants, they were given land, with the single proviso that if they did not till it properly they must yield it up to those who would. You see, it was outside the tenets of our creed to criticise anybody: we did not feel we had the right to do so.'

All the members of the community were more or less free of one another's houses. Nobody was allowed to suffer want. It was perhaps symbolical that everybody was called by his Christian name. All worked together towards one common end, and when work was finished they gathered together for the recreation of the mind or body by music and discussion and play. But now . . . my informant did not exactly say as much, but I inferred that things were quite different now.

'Then you admit that you have been defeated in your aim?' I asked. 'Not at all!' was the ready reply. 'I admit that conditions here today may not be what our original founders intended. I admit that there have had to be all sorts of adjustments and compromises during these latter years. I will even go so far as to admit that perhaps we have not proved quite what we originally set out to prove, namely, that it is possible to put the Tolstoyan ideal into practice.

'Other people have come along with other ideals which have sometimes clashed with ours. Yes, I admit all this, but I do not admit that we have been defeated. As individuals at least, I believe that we may claim to have preserved enough of the original ideal to justify the experiment. I even believe that we have given encouragement to others.'

In 1937, the year after Warren's publication of A COTSWOLD YEAR, that giant of Gloucestershire literature and prolific novelist John Moore gave the county a lasting love token with his book THE COTSWOLDS. To a general readership today he is best remembered for his Brensham Trilogy of novels, PORTRAIT OF ELMBURY, BRENSHAM VILLAGE and THE BLUE FIELD. But the people of the hills still know him best as the writer of perhaps the most lively and provocative book on the Cotswolds yet produced, a work that combined his intimate local knowledge with his considerable and not always happy experience of the greater world beyond.

Looking back over the ages it is significant that many of the more memorable writers about the Cotswolds have not been natives – or if they have been, they have at some stage distanced themselves from their native heath to hone their sense of perspective. 'What should they know of England who only England know?' Kipling asked, while closer to home, the Gloucestershire poet Leonard Clark once justified his living in London with the phrase: 'Absence is the grit in the oyster that produces the pearl'.

Moore's reflections are sharp and witty, and not always wholly what the natives wish to hear:

Cirencester has never ceased to be prosperous, has never felt the pinch of poverty, has only once – when Rupert stormed it and Essex retook it, in the Civil War – heard the clash of arms and the alarms of battle in its quiet sleepy streets. On that occasion the wealthy merchants, thinking of their bulging purses, took the Parliament side, and as usual in any matter touching their pockets they were right.

Cirencester's great and splendid church is a monument to these rich wool staplers, who largely rebuilt it in the fifteenth and sixteenth centuries; and in its very splendour one detects a sense of smugness and self-satisfaction. Read the epitaphs on the tombs and tablets, read of this merchant and that one whose virtue was that he went out of the world leaving riches behind him:

SEVEN NOBLES HE DID GIVE YE POORE FOR TO DEFEND
AND £80 TO XVII MEN DID LEND,
IN CISETER, BURFORD, ABINGDON AND TETBURIE
EVER TO BE TO THEM A STOCKE YERELY.

Well, they are gone, dust unto dust, the great merchants of wool. Here they lie, beneath the elaborate clerestories and the exquisite fan-tracery which they put up to the glory of God and to their own glory; here they lie, the Garstangs, who 'honoured' the Lady Chapel 'with worshipfull Vestimentis', Robert Rycarde, clothman, who left his 'scarlet and crimson gowne to be bestowed in vestures and ornaments to be used . . . to the lawde of God *and hym*,' Hugh Norres, grocer, and Johan hys wyf, 'Now dede in grave and beryed here, Yo' pryers desyring their soules for chere', Reginald Spycer amid his four wives, Margaretta, Juliana, Margarita and Johanna. Dust are they all, and their souls are fled, each to his own place, where their wealth may nothing avail them.

And the stupid sheep still feed and grow fat upon the Cotswold pastures; the descendants of those very sheep whose thick warm coats gave the merchants their riches. And Cirencester remains the wealthiest town in all Cotswold. Here you will find the biggest country houses, the most expensive motors, the most beautiful hunters, the best polo-ponies, the dullest society, and the most extravagant young women in Gloucestershire. It is even now as it was in Roman times; around Corinium Dobunorum rich men flourish like weeds.

Moore is also predictably sniffy about Bourton-on-the-Water, but there is something about Stow-on-the-Wold's bracing heights that appeals to him:

Bourton-on-the-Water is one of the 'show villages' of the Cotswolds; it is very neat and well-kept, and a little river spanned by bridges runs beside its street. (This is the same Windrush which gave me my kingfisher and my three-and-a-quarter pound trout at Burford.) Guide-books call Bourton 'the Cotswold Venice' and American visitors think it is very cute indeed; but the best of it has been destroyed, and its church is an abominable mixture of bogus Gothic superimposed on what was probably a delightful Georgian building.

Still, Bourton has a very nice cottage hospital (given to it, as a matter of fact, by my only rich relation, and named after him) and seems extremely proud of itself, in spite of the fact that it has ruined its church and destroyed its manor-houses and cut down its loveliest trees.

During the summer it lies in wait for American visitors. In the winter it counts up last year's takings and looks a bit smug, waiting for the next batch of visitors who will come, like the swallows, with the sun.

Very different is Stow-on-the-Wold. There is nothing bogus and nothing precious about it. It is honest and open-faced and does not try to be anything other than what it is: an old Cotswold market town, high up on the windy hills. They call it:

Stow-on-the-Wold
Where the devil caught cold,

and no wonder, for the wind whistles up the wide main street and through the market-place as keenly as it does up Princes Street in Edinburgh, and the devil, hot from his furnaces, must surely have wilted before that bitter blast. I have a private theory that, being angered by this chilly welcome, he decided to leave Stow severely alone and went off instead to Bourton-on-the-Water, where he counselled certain persons to restore the church of Saint Laurence – a good way of getting his own back on the Saint – and to Broadway, where he is still in residence,

Northleach

conducting a number of profitable businesses. But more of that later . . .

Stow at any rate has driven him away. Without any special airs and graces, it is nevertheless the perfect country town. Its grey stone houses are not 'show houses'; individually they are not strikingly beautiful and yet, with their blue or green doors and window frames and their weathered roofs of Cotswold tile, they are just right, they possess an air of having been there for ever. Bourton seems affected, Broadway is a parvenu, beside the quiet assurance of Stow-on-the-Wold. Walking through this street at dusk, I turned up my coat collar against the clean, buffeting wind, and felt grateful to that remembered wind for reminding me that I was back in the land of my fathers. It was nice to be home.

There is almost the spleen of William Cobbett in some of Moore's sentiments, and one shudders just slightly to think of what he might write about Stow today. The weather and the old grey streets have not changed much, but all those antique shops, the gift stores and cafes . . . could it be that the new era of weatherproof waxed jackets and central heating is giving the devil a foothold even here?

Having given Broadway the big build-up, we feel it would be cruel to deprive readers of Moore's unexpurgated reflections:

In its way Broadway is perfect; but so, after all, are most successful harlots.

It is sorrowfully observed by Juvenal that the agreement between beauty and modesty is extremely rare; and who shall blame Broadway, therefore, for marketing its beauty on a strictly commercial basis? Unfortunately Broadway does not confine itself to doing this. It is like the sort of harlot who not only charges you an exorbitant fee but seizes the opportunity of picking your pockets as well.

As I walked down the wide main street of Broadway in the dusk of this January afternoon I was aware that the inhabitants of the place were eyeing me through their windows and out of their shop doors with the kind of anticipatory eagerness of lions who watch a Christian walking into their den. I imagined them licking their lips and thinking: 'Not very fat, perhaps, but doubtless a forerunner of more and fatter Christians to come.'

It was not, heaven knows, that I had the appearance of a rich man; but the rucksack on my back was a sign and a symbol of returning spring. Seeing my rucksack, the people of Broadway stirred in their hibernacula, awakened from their slumber, and began to dream that the winter of their discontent was over at last.

One swallow does not make a spring, and one solitary hiker does not make a summer. But the swallow may be followed by two tomorrow, by twenty tomorrow week; and the hiker – who knows? – may be succeeded soon by others richer than he, by the first tourists in motor cars, by the gullible Americans themselves. More pockets to pick.

The shopkeepers smiled at me their Piccadilly smiles, so that I was reminded of the old nursery rhyme:

Will you come into my parlour?
Said the Spider to the Fly.

I smiled too, and walked on. I had been to Broadway before. I thought that I should like to write out a notice in big letters and carry it through Broadway on a sandwich-board, a notice like this:

I AM NOT AN AMERICAN OR A RICH IDIOT. I AM NOT INTERESTED IN SHAM ANTIQUES. I DO NOT REQUIRE ANY OF THOSE OLD OAK CHESTS WHICH YOU MAKE SO INGENIOUSLY. I ABOMINATE ALL MANIFESTATIONS OF ARTS-AND-CRAFTS. I AM NOT A FOLK-DANCER NOR A MORRIS-DANCER NOR A PLAYER UPON ANY KIND OF OBSOLETE MUSICAL INSTRUMENT. PLEASE DO NOT TRY TO SELL ME ANY HAND-WOVEN SCARVES. AND I DON'T WANT ANYTHING MADE OF RAFFIA EITHER. NOR DO I

WISH TO SIT ON A CHAIR WHICH WAS SAT ON BY QUEEN ELIZABETH OR TO SLEEP IN A BED WHICH WAS SLEPT IN BY KING CHARLES. ALL I WANT IS A PUB WITH A BAR WHERE I CAN BUY HALF-A-PINT OF DECENT BITTER FOR FOUR-PENCE AND TALK WITH HONEST MEN, IF THERE ARE ANY IN BROADWAY . . .

However, in its way Broadway is beautiful. And like any wise harlot it conserves its beauty with the utmost care. Even the petrol-pumps and the letter-boxes are painted in a non-committal shade; indeed they are so well camouflaged that it is almost impossible to find them when you run short of petrol or wish to post a letter.

Very ladylike, very genteel is Broadway; but so, of course, are all the best courtesans . . .

Moore obviously had a great deal of fun writing this, but today its barbs are somewhat blunted by period charm. Many other Cotswold centres have all but caught up with Broadway in terms of commercialisation now, and it would be pleasant if the modern tourist shop offered nothing more offensive than reproduction oak chests, Arts and Crafts goods, hand-woven scarves and raffia ware. In one particular, however, many of us can still agree with Moore: it *would* be nice to find a pub where you could buy half-a-pint of decent bitter for fourpence . . .

But good knockabout comedy as this is, it is no way in which to conclude our collage of images of this beautiful and most varied

corner of the country. Instead we turn to John Moore looking beyond the transient and the ephemeral, admiring the qualities that have shaped our region over a thousand years and more, and will continue to do so in the centuries ahead:

I don't suppose Elkstone Church is considered to be particularly beautiful; rather is it curious and interesting and quaint; yet it seemed to me, as I stood in its doorway this evening, to belong more truly to the Cotswolds, to be more a part of them, than the fine church at Northleach and John Tame's elaborate legacy to Fairford. Somehow this solid, unpretentious yet rather haunted-looking building, standing on the bleak, windswept uplands with an air of having been there for ever and of staying there for all future time, seemed to be typical of the whole Cotswold countryside . . .

I felt, as I stood here in the dusk, that I had found one certainty among a confusion of uncertainties; and that if in the next few years we make a shambles of the world, and if I survive it, I shall be able to come back here knowing surely that I shall see the tall, square tower on its windy hill, and the little homesteads that have grown out of the very earth huddled about it, and the sheep still pastured between the grey stone walls, and a ploughman, more patient even than his slow, patient horse, driving a straight furrow down the slope towards Colesbourne.

Acknowledgements

We would like to thank the following for kindly allowing us to reproduce copyright material in the text: Dr John Harvey; Dr Alison Hanham; the Estate of C. Henry Warren; Mr. M.W. Thompson & South Glamorgan County Library; Mr Francis Witts; Mrs Rosemary Verey; the Estate of Mrs D.E. Hall; Mr Laurie Lee; and finally Mrs Lucile Bell. For permission to use the quotations on the dust jacket we thank Mr P.J. Kavanagh; the Estate of Alec Clifton-Taylor; and Victor Gollancz Limited. For general advice and assistance with the book we thank Mr. R.N. Dore; Mr P.W. Hammond; and Mr David Viner. Finally, we thank Mrs Jill Voyce and the staff of the Gloucestershire Local History Collection at Gloucester City Library.

The credits and information on all of the illustrations used in this book are given in page ascending sequence. Where a source is referred to frequently, only initials are used, and the key to these is at the base of the page. The sepia-reproduced photographs are not dated, but most fall into a time span of 1890 to 1920, with a few either side of these dates. Counties are only given when they are not Gloucestershire.

Page 2 Upper Cam, *D.E.E.*; 3 Stanton, *Packer Collection, Oxfordshire County Museum*; 4 Map of Gloucestershire by Johannes Kip, from Sir Robert Atkyn's *The Ancient and Present State of Glostershire*, 1712; 6 Chalford, *D.E.*; 7 Sezincote, *R.C.*; 8 Cerney House, *S. & B.*; 10 Condicote Lane, *B.M.*; 11 A Cotswold barn near Northleach, *P.F*; 12 Fifteenth-century mercenary soldiers; 14 Summer flowers near Calmsden, *P.F.*; 15 Horses running in a field at Cowley, *P.F.*; 17 Small detail from an engraving, *S. & B.*; 18 Owlpen Manor near Uley, *J.B.*; 19 Northleach, *C.C.C.*; 20 Brass in Northleach Church; 21 Detail from Ogilby's *Road Maps of England and Wales* 1675; 22 Haymaking on a Cotswold estate at Batsford, *C.C.C.*; 23 The blacksmith's shop at Stockend, Harescombe, *G.R.O.*; 26 Ludgate Hill, Wotton-under-Edge, *D.E.*; 27 High Street, Wotton-under-Edge, *D.E.*; 29 Detail from a view of Gloucester, *Buck N.W.P.*; 30 Master and his gamekeeper after a rabbit shoot, *C.C.C.*; 31 A cold morning, high in the Cotswolds, *P.F.*; 34 Berkeley Castle, *R.N.*; 35 Bagendon, *P.F.*; 38 Dursley from Broadway, *R.C.*; 39 Painswick lychgate, *J.B.*; 42 Compton Abdale, *P.F.*; 43 'A rest by the way' . . . three farm workers taking a rest from their labours, *C.C.C.*; 46 The War Memorial, Northleach, *C.C.C.*; 47 The Market House, Tetbury, *D.E.*; 48 Captain Dover's Games, *Annalia Dubrensia*; 50 Bringing home the orphan, *C.C.C.*; 51 The village ford, Taynton, *C.C.C.*; 53 Speed's map of Gloucester as reproduced in Fosbrooke's *Original History of the City of Gloucester*; 54 Little Wolford near Shipston-on-Stour, *C.C.C.*; 55 A winter view of Painswick, *B.M.*; 56 Early seventeenth-century woodcut of a canoneer; 57 Title page from Colonel Morgan's letter; 58 Stow-on-the-Wold, *P.F.*; 59 Burford, *P.F.*; 62 The ruins of Minster Lovell Hall, *J.B.*; 63 Sheepscombe, *R.N.*; 65 Detail from a view of Gloucester, *Buck N.W.P.*; 66 The Old Mill House,

Frampton Mansell, *P.F.*; 67 A call from the miller, *C.C.C.*; 68 Dursley parish church, as engraved by Thomas Bonnor in 1782 for Bigland's *Historical, Monumental, and Genealogical Collections Relative to the County of Gloucester*; 70 Parsonage Street, Dursley, *D.E.E.*; 71 Parsonage Street and Market House, Dursley, *D.E.E.*; 72 Thornbury Castle, *S. & B.*; 74 Arlington Mill, Bibury, *C.C.C.*; 75 Swan Hotel, Bibury, *C.C.C.*; 76 Bourton-on-the-Water, *G.C.*; 77 Market Place, Cirencester, *S. & B.*; 78 A farmyard at Coln St. Dennis, *M.E.R.L.*; 79 Bourton-on-the-Water, *R.N.*; 82 The River Coln at Fairford, *P.F.*; 83 The River Leach and bridge at Eastleach, *P.F.*; 84 River Frome and Eastington House, *S. & B.*; 86 Broadway, *P.F.*; 87 Stanton, *J.B.*; 90 Arlington Row, Bibury, *J.B.*; 91 Arlington Row, Bibury, *C.C.C.*; 94 Workers in the hayfield on the Wantage estate at Lockinge, Berkshire, *M.E.R.L.*; 95 Three-horse team, turning on the headland, *C.C.C.*; 96 Detail from engraving of Rendcombe, *S. & B.*; 97 Further detail from engraving of Rendcombe, *S. & B.*; 98 Tetbury, *D.E.*; 99 Painswick, *D.E.*; 100 Gloucester docks basin, *S. & B.*; 101 An engraving from S.Y. Griffith's *A Historical Description of Cheltenham*; 102 The Chipping Steps, Tetbury, *D.E.*; 103 The Thames & Severn Canal at Coates, *P.F.*; 104 Fairford Church, *S. & B.*; 105 A general view of Cheltenham from Griffith's *Cheltenham*; 106 A cornfield near Chedworth, *P.F.*; 107 The Devil's Chimney, Leckhampton, *B.M.*; 108 An engraving from Griffith's *Cheltenham*; 109 Chevenage House, *S. & B.*; 110 Dollar Street, Cirencester, *J.B.*; 111 The Thames & Severn Canal at the Golden Valley, *P.F.*; 112 Sudeley Castle, and engraving from Samuel Rudder's *New History of Gloucestershire*; 114 The Rollright Stones, *B.M.*; 115 The yard of the King's Arms Hotel, Stow-on-the-Wold, *C.C.C.*; 118 Two young carters at Little Tew, Oxfordshire, *C.C.C.*; 119 Condicote, *C.C.C.*; 120 Cirencester churchyard, *S. & B.*; 121 An engraving from Griffith's *Cheltenham*; 122 Relaxation after work, *C.C.C.*; 123 Dean Row, Coln St. Aldwyn, *C.C.C.*; 125 Prinknash Park, *S. & B.*; 126 John Brinkworth, hedger and ditcher, *M.E.R.L.*; 127 A stone wall near Yanworth, *P.F.*; 130 Westonbirt Arboretum, *R.N.*; 131 Autumn scene at Lower Slaughter, *J.B.*; 134 Wild flowers in a cornfield at Chedworth, *P.F.*; 135 Hampnett, *P.F.*; 137 Gatcombe Park, *S. & B.*; 138 Upper Slaughter, *P.F.*; 139 Nailsworth, *C.C.C.*; 141 Westgate Street, Gloucester, *S. & B.*; 142 The village smithy, Kingham, Oxfordshire, *C.C.C.*; 143 Shearing sheep by hand, *C.C.C.*; 146 The Old Elm Tree, Bishop's Cleeve, *Tim Curr*; 147 Monk's Mill, Alderley, *D.E.*; 148 St. Mary's Mill, Chalford, *G.C.*; 150 Painswick, *D.E.*; 151 Hidcote Manor, *P.F.*; 152 Bowden Hall, Upton St. Leonards, *S. & B.*; 154 Naunton, *R.N.*; 155 View of Gloucester from the north-west, *S. & B.*; 156 Long Street, Dursley, a view from Blunt's *Dursley and its Neighbourhood*; 158 Bisley, *B.M.*; 159 Swan Hotel, Bibury, *J.B.*; 162 Yanworth, *P.F.*; 163 The Trout Inn, Lechlade, *C.C.C.*; 164 Detail from the engraving of Boxwell Court, *S. & B.*; 165 Williamstrip, *S. & B.*; 166 Two men in a field of stooked hay at Cherington, *C.C.C.*; 167 Threshing at University Farm, Hailey, near Witney, Oxfordshire, *C.C.C.*; 170 A village feast at Stretton-on-Fosse, Warwickshire, *C.C.C.*; **171** Thompson's Bakery, Sherston, *D.E.*; **174** Cirencester Mop, *Gloucestershire County Library, Bingham Library, Cirencester*; **178** Snowshill, *P.F.*; **182** A river bank near Southrop, *P.F.*; **183** St. Peter's Church, Winchcombe, *J.B.*; **187** The Red Lion at Northleach, *C.C.C.*

Key to initials: B.M. *Bill Meadows*; Buck N.W.P. *The North West Prospect of the City of Gloucester, by George and Nathaniel Buck, 1734*; C.C.C. *Cotswold Countryside Collection, Northleach (Corinium Museum, Cirencester)*; D.E. *Donald Emes*; D.E.E. *David E. Evans*; G.C. *Gloucestershire Collection, Gloucester City Library*; G.R.O. *Gloucestershire Record Office*; J.B. *John Blake*; M.E.R.L. *Museum of English Rural Life, Reading*; P.F. *Paul Felix*; R.C. *Robert Carr*; R.N. *Roy Nash*; S. & B. *J. & H.S. Storer and J.N. Brewer, Delineations of Gloucestershire, 1826.*

Bibliography

Baddeley, Welbore St. Claire; *A Cotteswold Manor*, 1929.

Bibliotheca Gloucestrensis: A Collection of Scarce and Curious Tracts, Relating to the County and City of Gloucester; Illustrative of, and Published During the Civil War, 1823.

Birchall, Dearman; *The Diary of a Victorian Squire*, edited by David Verey, 1983.

Blunt, John Henry; *Dursley and its Neighbourhood*, 1877.

Calvertt, John Simpson; *Rain and Ruin, the Diary of an Oxfordshire Farmer, 1875–1900*, edited by Celia Miller, 1983.

Cely, (Cely family & correspondents); *The Cely Letters 1472–1488*, edited by Alison Hanham, Early English Text Society no. 273, 1975.

Cobbett, William; *Rural Rides in Surrey, Kent and other Counties*, 2 vols. 1853.

Herbert, Nicholas; *Road Travel and Transport in Gloucestershire*, 1985.

Colt Hoare, Sir Richard; *The Journeys of Sir Richard Colt Hoare through Wales and England 1793–1810*, edited by M.W. Thompson, 1983.

Defoe, Daniel; *A Tour through the Whole Island of Great Britain*, 1753.

The Dictionary of National Biography.

Gibbs, J. Arthur; *A Cotswold Village*, 1899.

Gloucestershire Notes and Queries, vols. I to VII, edited by B.H. Blacker and W.P.W. Phillimore, 1881 – 1900.

Journal of the House of Lords, vol. 8.

Kilvert, Francis; *Kilvert's Diary 1870–1879*, edited by William Plomer, 3 vols. 1940.

Lee, Laurie; *Cider with Rosie*, 1959.

Leland, John; *The Itinerary of John Leland 1535–1543*, edited by Lucy Toulmin Smith, 4 vols. 1907–1910.

Marshall, William; *The Rural Economy of Glocestershire*, 1789.

Miles, W.A.; *Report on the Condition of Hand Loom Weavers in Gloucestershire*, 1839.

Moore, John; *The Cotswolds*, 1937.

The Oxford English Dictionary.

Peck, Francis; *Collection of Divers Curious Historical Pieces*, 1740.

Plot, Robert; *The Natural History of Oxfordshire*, 1676.

Rudder, Samuel; *A New History of Gloucestershire*, 1779.

Shakespeare, William; *The Complete Works.*

Smith, John; *Men and Armour for Gloucestershire in 1608*, 1902.

Smith [Smyth], John; *A Description of the Hundred of Berkeley*, edited by Sir John Maclean, 1885.

Southey, Robert; *Letters from England*, 1807.

Temple Thurston, Ernest; *The Flower of Gloster*, 1911.

Walpole, Horace; *Selected Letters*, selected and edited by William Hadley, 1926.

Warren, C. Henry; *A Cotswold Year*, 1936.

Witts, Reverend F.E.; *The Diary of a Cotswold Parson*, edited by David Verey, 1978.

Worcestre, William; *William Worcestre Itineraries*, edited by John H. Harvey, 1969.

Index

COUNTRY LIFE SERIES
IN THE HAY